101 SPORTS NOT TO TRY

101 SPORTS Not TO TRY

PORTICO

First published in the United Kingdom in 2008 by
Portico Books
10 Southcombe Street
London
W14 0RA

An imprint of Anova Books Company Ltd

ISBN 10: 1-906032-64-5
ISBN 13: 978-1-906032-64-7

Picture credits for cover:
Front cover: Corbis
Back cover: Troy Kennedy/iStockphoto (Sumo), Olaf Loose/iStockphoto
(Grandstand)

A CIP catalogue record for this book is available from the British Library.

Main text: Adam Russ
Panel text: Martin Howard and Andrew Davies
Captions: Andrew Davies
Picture research: Theo Hopkinson
Designer: Cara Rodgers

10 9 8 7 6 5 4 3 2 1

Reproduction by Rival Colour Ltd.
Printed and bound by Print Communications Pte Ltd, Singapore

This book can be ordered direct from the publisher.
Contact the marketing department, but try your bookshop first.

www.anovabooks.com

Introduction

Got plans for the weekend? No? Well why not try re-plumbing your bathroom? OK, if that doesn't appeal, how about stripping the engine of your car? Not for any particular reason, of course – just for the sheer joy of stripping your engine and then failing to put it back together properly.

We all have our strengths and weaknesses, and with any luck whoever puts money in your bank account every month doesn't do it out of pity. Hopefully, those credits appear every month because you have

something to offer. And every now and then you do more than just offer. You deliver. The things we're not good at are best left to professionals. Plumbers, mechanics, orthodontists, teachers, and yes, even policemen, receive training on how to plumb, fix, extract, educate and arrest respectively. We wouldn't dream of attempting to do their jobs in our spare time, and certainly not for fun.

And yet every weekend, a collective hysteria descends across the planet. From Birmingham to Bora Bora, Sydney to Santiago, Helsinki to Hell's

One of the hazards of the Pamplona run is camera-hogging bulls.

Never play street hockey with nuns. They *know* they have God on their side.

"Okay, who moved the landing stage..."

Kitchen, normal, everyday folk put on loud, tight-fitting clothing, apply straps and supports to their saggy frames like medals of honour, stop at the corner store for sugary drinks they wouldn't touch if they weren't labelled "isotonic" and indulge themselves in the fantasy that they are sporty. They aren't. And if that sounds like you, it's time for a reality check. Whatever its origins, sport in the twenty-first century is big business.

Sport is for professionals. Accept it. Spend your weekends gardening, decorating, whatever fills the void in your existence in whatever way suits you best. But under no circumstances indulge in a once-a-week exercise in what might have been if you'd decided against taking the job in computing and followed your dream of being a professional rodeo rider/squash player/synchronised swimmer. The pros are there for us to worship for the modern gods they truly are. In a society where we've all but lost any sense of what religion is, it's worth remembering that a spot of non-competitive donkey riding aside, Jesus didn't do sports. But his holy father did make everything in the world, and hence plasma screen TVs. And thumbs to press the remote control with. Of course much is made of the money professional sportsmen and women earn today, but that's down to what the market will bear. Many will argue that it is obscene for Ferrari's Kimi Raikkonen to earn a salary believed to be around $52m a year – $1m in a single week. And he can go to a grand prix and stuff it into the gravel trap at the third corner and still pick up his cheque.

But sit in a Formula One car and steam down the straight at Mount Fuji in the pouring rain at 300kph with no visibility and try and pick your braking point and you realise that this guy has balls of diamantine. So the major entertainment sports should be handled by the professionals. The rest are best left to extroverts, perverts and geography teachers. As we will find out...

3-Day Eventing

At its best, 3-day eventing shows the remarkable links that can exist between a well-bred, but essentially stupid, creature and the horse that they sit on top of.

Country of Origin: France

Possibility of death or serious injury: Far greater than motor racing, actually.

Embarrassing clothing: Oh yes, riders need three sets of attire; one for each day of the event. The best bit of all is the dressage section, when riders have to kit themselves out in top hats and frock coats like they're in a Jane Austen novel and are riding over to Pemberley to see Mr. Darcy.

Greatest hazard: The horse having second thoughts that this is such a great idea, especially when it's asked to jump into water or over a series of brightly coloured poles.

Prize/Rewards: The sort of silverware that will keep Jeeves and his tub of Brasso busy all year. Big rosettes too.

People most likely to enjoy it: If you have buck teeth, no chin and an Adam's apple that sticks out further than your nose, this could be the sport for you.

Potential expansion: There are plans to create 4-day eventing by adding an extra event – beer dray pulling – to appeal to a wider demographic.

Expect to hear: "Has Lucinda gorne into the water...?"

a journey which can now be completed in about four hours with any budget airline. It's seen as one of the few truly unifying Olympic events – not only can women and men actually compete with each other, but, given its popularity with the royal families of Europe, chances are they're also related. Whilst the discipline originated in France, 3-day eventing was named and pretty much adopted by the British. In 1949 they made the combination of dressage, cross country fences and show-jumping the centrepiece of the somewhat misleadingly named Badminton Horse Trials (no shuttlecocks were involved and the only cross examination was to check for lameness on Sunday morning).

You'll Need…

A horse. Any breed will do, although given the chance of it landing on your head, the lighter and more good natured the better. You'll also need three sets of riding attire for each of the different disciplines. Conservative riding dress should be donned for cross-country, more traditional formal wear is expected for show-jumping, though an armband containing

You can lead a horse to water, but you can't make it jump over difficult stuff.

History

Another in the seemingly endless series of sports with roots in military history, 3-day eventing was originally designed as an intense test for cavalry mounts, culminating in a 72-hour, 360-mile ride from Vienna to Berlin;

medical history and last will and testament remains a requirement. Dressage may be the least hazardous part of the contest in terms of physical harm, but you're still running the risk of a mauling by the equine fashion police if you or your horse puts a foot wrong. A shadbelly can be worn but only if it is accompanied by a top hat. The kind of smug, superior expression you'd expect to see on someone who admits to owning a top hat, or even knowing what a shadbelly is, will of course be mandatory throughout.

How You Do It

Dressage, as the dress code implies, is all about poncing around. Show jumping is slightly less dangerous than cross country, where courses are designed to push horse and rider to the limit. Only the most skilled riders can hope to complete a round with minimal penalties. However, members of the upper class not in possession of the required degree of equine expertise can recreate the thrills and spills of this most challenging of horsey pursuits simply by having their butler tie them to the underside of a grand piano and launch them over the banisters at their country estate.

Advanced

At its best, 3-day eventing shows the remarkable links that can exist between a well-bred, but essentially stupid, creature and the horse that they sit on top of. The truly great eventers will always remember that they are only one bad jump away from having their backbones lovingly squashed by the heavier half of the partnership. As a result their devotion to their steeds is conveyed in language that defies description. If you regard describing a creature with the profile of a pre-surgery Cher and the odour of a compost heap as "pretty headed and a real sweet natured push button" then it may just be that 3-day eventing is for you.

Why You Shouldn't Bother

Despite its genteel image, 3-day eventing has claimed more lives in the last year than F1, downhill skiing, or appearing on TV shows featuring Simon Cowell.

In moves to make the sport more popular with the kids on the street, the Brazilian government have introduced the Sao Paulo Horse Trials – the Favella Classic – with a modified final day to include evasion riding techniques.

Air Racing

With certain death awaiting any small mistake it's difficult to understand why anyone in their right mind would take up air racing. One inadvertent slip of the joystick and that's it – you've bought the farm.

Country of Origin: USA

Possibility of death or serious injury: Yes, the sharing nature of the air race means that both participants and spectators are equally at risk.

Embarrassing clothing: Flight suits that make pilots look like they're in a 1980s synthesizer duo from Sheffield.

Greatest hazard: Without wishing to state the bleedin' obvious, screaming out of the sky at hundreds of miles an hour with only a crowd of spectators to break your fall.

People most likely to enjoy it: Nutters who are good with engines.

Don't expect to hear: "Tora, tora, tora!"

Proposals by Russian pilots to add "strafing" to the first timed run have been rejected.

History

Like a kid with a new toy, it wasn't long after the aircraft was invented that man was looking for ways to do new and interesting things with it. Strapping on guns and dropping bombs out of it certainly made World War I go with a bang, and having chorus lines of girls dancing along the wings in the 1920s made the early days of commercial air travel more interesting for the passengers. It's generally acknowledged that the first event in air racing history took place during the Grand Week of Champagne in Reims, France and led for calls to the authorities to introduce legislation on drink-flying, which were roundly ignored by everyone, especially the French. The history of air racing thereafter was characterised by the rise of a given event attached to a given city until engine failure, pilot error or a building led to the inevitable fatalities, and hefty insurance claims.

You'll Need...

A major league sponsor. The big one these days is Red Bull, though they won't actually give you any wings.

Why You Shouldn't Bother

Most of the pilots competing in the big air races have clocked up more hours flight time than an EasyJet stewardess. And they still have accidents.

Air racers are often plagued by poor engine maintenance.

American Football

It's a great sport indeed that provides has-been pop stars with the opportunity to brandish their still-edgy street credentials before a family audience, only to hastily claim they hadn't meant to be so edgy or street the next day and that it was all some wardrobe assistant's fault.

Country of Origin: USA

Possibility of death or serious injury: Some, but not as much as you'd like.

Embarrassing clothing: By wearing the equivalent of an Abrahams tank for a sport that everyone else plays in a pair of shorts and a shirt, if they're not embarrassed, they damn well should be.

Greatest hazard: Fondling the quarterback's butt a little too often before "the snap" and getting a taste for it.

Prize/Rewards: You see those cheerleaders…

People most likely to enjoy it: Anyone with an attention span of twenty seconds or less, the time it takes to run a play and then cut to the adverts.

Potential expansion? No. The rest of the world prefers to see rugby players playfully grinding each other's heads into the mud and turf.

Expect to hear: "We'll be right back after these messages."

History

Invented as a means of selling beer kegs, 3kg bags of potato chips and cable TV subscriptions, American football shares a number of features with other sports popular around the rest of the world. It's a lot like rugby union, except that players are permitted to pass the ball forwards. It shares with rugby league a limit to the number of tackles a team can take before losing possession of the ball, although in rugby league it's six to American football's four. And it has all the intense physicality of Australian rules football, albeit with a great deal more padding. One major distinction between these two sports is that Aussie rules draws its players from a gene pool that's rich in criminal ex-pat Brits, yet produces remarkably few law breakers. American football meanwhile has become something of a breeding ground for the previously law-abiding to learn questionable behaviour, with tax evasion, animal cruelty and being found not guilty of murdering your pretty blonde wife, the favourite causes for brushing with the law in recent years.

You'll Need…

About 100 mates. Per team. Gridiron is the world's leading team sport for specialised positions, with a role for everyone from wide receivers (for fast runners with good hands) to kickers (for good kickers, naturally) and

Kickers are usually small and girlish and get changed on their own.

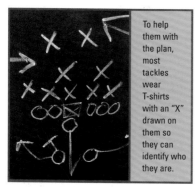

To help them with the plan, most tackles wear T-shirts with an "X" drawn on them so they can identify who they are.

defensive linemen (for enormous salad dodgers who wouldn't get picked to play in any other team in any other sport anywhere in the world except maybe pie eating, or sumo). You'll also need enough body armour to keep the LAPD protected for ten years of rioting, a long tape measure strung between two poles, a platoon of middle-aged men dressed in black and white stripes and a ball.

How You Do It

Despite a relatively simple rule book, American football has probably produced more literature, debate and commentary than any other sport in history. Each side will comprise three distinct teams for offense, defense and special plays, and will collectively be expected to learn

hundreds of set plays in order to succeed. All of which can make American football one of the most satisfying sports in the world from a spectator's perspective. Taking the maxim that you can get too much of a good thing, the sport's governing bodies have conspired with broadcasters to ensure that viewers don't overindulge in the richness of the sport by ensuring that for every minute's worth of actual action they get to watch they'll also have to endure ten minutes' worth of commercials. Since it is a stop-start affair, this can mean that a game with an hour's scheduled playtime takes six hours to complete. This reaches its apogee on Super Bowl Sunday, when advertisers pay top dollar for a chance to mainline directly into the majority of American homes, not to mention a growing number of international ones.

Why You Shouldn't Bother

For those wishing to play without spending the GNP of a small country, a version of the game exists where the objective is effectively the same but team size is severely reduced and physical contact is all but outlawed. This is referred to by Americans as "touch football" and by everyone else as "Piggie in the Middle". Apart from in the U.S., it is generally played by little girls of a sensitive disposition.

The center awaits for the warm and comforting touch of his quarterback as he prepares to shout vital numbers followed by the mandatory "hut, hut hut!"

Angling

Despite the huge popularity of the sport worldwide, angling remains a largely male pursuit, and most anglers will admit that a large part of their passion is the peace that their sport offers them. Peace from work, peace from their fellow man, and – above all – peace from the wife.

Country of Origin: Unknown

Possibility of death or serious injury: Very high when fishing next to high-tension electricity cables.

Embarrassing clothing: It depends what your view on rubber waders is. Some people would pay money, etc.

Greatest hazards: Getting hooked, getting battered by an angry swan, getting struck by lightning.

Prize/Rewards: Hours of peace and the beauty of watching the sun come up over the misty, limpid waters of the canal.

People most likely to enjoy it: Melancholic beta males who need to dominate a small, stupid, defenceless animal.

Expect to hear: "Still nothing yet...?"

History

Since the dawn of time, man has pitted himself against nature. Sought to climb the highest, most remote and treacherous peaks on the planet. Thrown himself at the mercy of raging seas in quests of exploration. And pitted his wits against the most sly and cunning creatures in all God's creation, from ferocious wild cats to savage giant bears and...fish. Yes, outwitting a creature with a seven-second memory has rapidly become the world's number one sport that involves killing or injuring creatures, largely because no one can quite be bothered to take up the cause of an animal that's cold, scaly and scary looking, and which frankly only seems to be serving its true life purpose when it's been filleted, lightly seared and served up with a dash of lemon juice and a few capers.

You'll Need...

The kit you require all depends on how far you'll need to go to in order to convince the woman in your life that you're participating in a worthwhile and serious activity. And how long you want to be as far from her as possible. In the most simple cases, you'll need a roach pole, a bit of live bait, something to sit on, bus fare for a trip and above all alcohol to numb the tedium. If your relationship is on shakier ground and you need some serious space then deep sea fishing might be the answer, involving as it will a much earlier start, the extra expense of chartering a boat and the added bonus of a nice big padded leather chair for you to get drunk in while you wait for your little aquatic quarries to bite. In truly terminal cases rock fishing is probably the answer, as this has the highest recorded casualty numbers year on year, thus offering you the chance to extend your time out from life to include a lengthy hospital stay or even a one-way trip to the bottom of the ocean.

Just as anglers can delude themselves that the big fish is out there, waiting to be caught, so they believe that one day this will happen.

What a catch! All day sat at the side of a dismal lake with $1,000 of fishing equipment and then this little monster comes out of the deep to make it all worthwhile.

How You Do It

Get up early. Find water. Bait hook. Cast off. Drink beer. Sleep for eight hours.

Advanced

The big debate in recent years in angling circles has been over an issue that won't concern new anglers, namely what to do with any fish that actually get caught. In competitive circles, catch-and-release has become accepted practice, but there are arguments that this makes the act of tricking a creature to impale itself on a barbed hook not that sporting at all. This lobby would prefer the fish to be killed. Either way you can't help but feel the fish aren't really getting represented. But then, they don't deserve to. They're fish.

Why You Shouldn't Bother

While fish are wondrous in their variety, tasty in the extreme and a fantastic source of omega oils, they are not, have never been, and never will be, wily opponents. The evidence for their not being up to the task of outwitting human opponents is to be witnessed in the ice-packed nativity scene of piscine ineptitude on show in every high-street supermarket and seafood restaurant on the planet.

NO CAST NETTING
OR SNATCH HOOKING OF MULLET

To be honest, the chance of hooking some snatch whilst smelling like a fishmonger's waste bin is very remote indeed.

Arm Wrestling

Arm Wrestling in the USA is a serious business, with weight divisions, syndicated slots on ESPN and a cast of thick-necked, buzz cut characters as diverse, dynamic and charismatic as a box of used toothpicks.

Country of Origin: Egypt

Possibility of death or serious injury: No. But you could end up with a dislocated shoulder, torn ligaments, burst blood vessels, bruised knuckles or even a fractured humerus.

Embarrassing clothing: Brightly coloured handkerchiefs tied round the head and sweaty vests are popular – aka "the Bruce Willis look".

Greatest hazard: Sweaty palms.

Prize/Rewards: Get really good and there's a chance that you might get to endorse Mr. Muscle.

People most likely to enjoy it: Body builders with a low IQ (though some might say that goes with the territory), plus sportsmen and women with a high percentage of Cromagnon genes – typically nose tackles from U.S. football.

Expect to hear: "Grrrrrrrrrrrgggg, Hrrggg, Grrrrrrrraaaaaaaaaagggggggggg!"

History

Arm wrestling may well have been around before the ancient Egyptians, but as usual they were the first people to make pictures of it – Ramesses versus Darius was *the* bout of the third millennium BC. Four thousand years later, the Americans wrote a rulebook for it, formed an organisation to market the sport and claimed it as their own.

You'll Need...

Champion arm wrestler "Snoopy" discovered to his cost and ultimate disqualification in the World Wrist wrestling Championships at Petaluma in 1968, that having an arm is not enough – you need a human hand too, and specifically a thumb which you can lock into your opponent's. You'll also need a flat surface. You could do it on the floor, a clutter-free table is better, best of all is one of the pro arm wrestling tables that come with nifty features like grips for your free arm and padded circular areas for competitors' elbows.

How You Do It

While arm wrestling may look truck-drivingly simple, there is slightly more to it than meets the eye. Pro Arm Wrestlers argue that while the general perception is that their sport is all about upper body strength, it's about 80 per cent mental. Leaving aside the impression most outsiders have that the sport is actually 100 per cent mental, there does certainly seem to be a lot of sense in going into any bout with a kick-ass attitude, despite the fact that actual ass kicking is strictly prohibited under WAF rules. Not to mention very difficult from the other side of a table.

Advanced

Once you've learnt the basics – gripping your opponent's hand with thumbs locked and then pushing until you've pinned their arm down – you'll be ready to learn the advanced strategies that lie behind this fascinating and complex sport... such as not letting go of your opponent's hand, as this will constitute a foul. Not letting him push *your* arm down, as this will constitute losing. And questioning the degree of hairiness of your opponent's mother and the sexual appetite of his wife during the longer bouts.

Australian Rules Football

A game so bloodthirsty, brutal and spectacularly entertaining it wouldn't have looked out of place if it was played on the supporting bill in a Roman arena – just after the Gladiators, just before the Lions versus Christians.

History

If imitation is the sincerest form of flattery then you'd have to say that deep down Australians really do have a crushingly deep infatuation with their British cousins. For most of its history the imaginative folk of the U.K. have been inventing sports for the rest of the world to play, modifying the rules as and when they saw fit in order to maintain some kind of ability to, if not dominate, then, at least hold their own.

And while the Australian nation has proved incredibly adept at beating the Brits at all these games – whether that game be cricket, rugby or, God help us, even soccer – then you have to mark them down for thinking it would be easy to come up with a game of their own that they could beat the rest of the world at. But that's exactly what they've tried with Australian rules football, a sport that combines the brute violence of bare-knuckle cage fighting with the

Ice cream sellers double as goal-line referees in Aussie rules. Here, one of the vendors signals to the other end that he has sold out of choc-ices and is running low on toffee cheesecake Cornettos.

silky ball control skills of cross-country running. All in aid of a game that's watched by a worldwide audience that's rapidly approaching triple figures.

You'll Need...

A team of 18 players may seem a little excessive, but you will be covering an oval pitch that could be 185m in length and 155m across – which in midday Antipodean heat will be no laughing matter. All but the uber fit will be dropping like flies, and that's before you've even had the pleasure of acquainting yourselves with the opposing team. You'll need a sleeveless top known as a Guernsey, a gumshield for holding your teeth in your mouth even after they've been pounded out of their sockets, and padding for your ickle-wickle limbs only if you want to be accused of being a total pussy by every other player on the field, as well as everyone in the crowd. Including your mum.

How You Do It

To many first time viewers, a game of Australian rules football can seem incredibly confusing, and it will leave the viewer mystified as to what tactics the two teams have employed in their attempts to win the game. More experienced viewers of the action are beyond supposing anything as sophisticated as a "tactic" is employed.

Advanced

Looking to inject a further gratuitous level of violence into an already 18-certificate sport, throwing has been outlawed from Aussie rules since its inception. Players are instead expected to punch the ball, which is coyly referred to as "hand passing". You may take some comfort from the fact that the ball is the one thing you'll encounter that won't be throwing any punches back at you.

Why You Shouldn't Bother

The Aussie rules community are passionate about their sport and an invitation to play may well be hard to refuse. Should you be unlucky

"I have three Zooms left. Shall I bring them over at half-time?"

enough to get involved in one of these limb-crushing fests the main thing to remember is not to question or challenge the rules of the game. Accept that your time on the pitch will be a slightly more intense version of a trip into the Aussie outback – you'll be running around hopelessly in a seemingly endless dustbowl bereft of any signs of life, other than the wide collection of mean-looking dangerous animals whose sole purpose is to do you serious harm... But you will get a good tan.

Country of Origin: New Zealand. Just kidding.

Possibility of death or serious injury: Very much the game's major attraction.

Embarrassing clothing: Any kind of protective gear is for those of a less-than-fully-heterosexual persuasion.

Greatest hazard: From the simple punch in the face to having a human bulldozer jumping up and down on your cranium, the hazards of Australian football are almost endless.

Prize/Rewards: The sheer joy of still clinging to life when it's all over briefly outweighs the fact that you'll be eating food from a blender from now on.

People most likely to enjoy it: Anyone not actually involved in playing it.

Potential expansion: There's talk of arming the teams with machetes.

Expect to hear: "I want a good clean fight. I mean match."

Badminton

The blue riband event of the limp-wristed Olympiad, the game of badminton has all the macho appeal of a trip to the cinema to see *Mamma Mia!* It's the game of choice for sex offenders and geography teachers alike.

Country of Origin: Japan

Possibility of death or serious injury: Only if double-booked on the sports centre's basketball court.

Embarrassing clothing: Yes, it's a sport beloved of geography teachers who insist on wearing their John McEnroe headbands (circa 1977) even though the hair it's supposedly keeping out of their eyes disappeared with Wham! in the 1980s.

People most likely to enjoy it: Those for whom a tennis racquet is just too achingly heavy.

Potential expansion: Yeah, right.

Fascinating fact: Many British children are forced to try badminton at school by sadistic games teachers and cope with the ordeal by trying to lodge the shuttlecock as high as possible in the sports hall roof.

After the game expect to hear: "Hey, everyone back to my place for a Baileys and ice."

An enthusiastic badminton player awaits service.

History

The term "metrosexual" was coined in the 1990s by popular columnist and commentator Mark Simpson to describe a man confident in exhibiting peacock tendencies in his manner of dress, grooming and lifestyle choices. Icons of masculinity don't play badminton citing the well-argued position that it's "far too gay".

You'll Need...

Badminton shoes are lightweight, laterally streamlined for increased mobility, and as terminally uncool as everything else associated with this unfortunate sport.

How You Do It

Players stand on opposing sides of the net, and the server hits the shuttlecock. Play continues until the shuttlecock goes out of play by touching the ground. This will happen within 6–10 seconds of the service at a professional level. At novice level you can expect it to happen within 30–35 minutes.

Advanced

The world's best players will employ a wide repertoire of shots (including "net kill", the "jump smash" and the "spinning netshot") and are capable of achieving speeds of more than 200mph with their goose-feather shuttlecocks. New players are more likely to find themselves using the more traditional "knock it up in the air for the other player to return" they learnt on the beach 20 years ago from their parents. You're unlikely to generate much speed on a cheap nylon shuttlecock. Rather than wasting money on expensive equipment you might want to find an alternative. Like a dead sparrow.

Bare-knuckle Fighting

Try to hurt your opponent. Try not to be hurt by him. Exploit his weak points and try not to let him know where yours are. It's a lot like a marriage, but with a great deal more physical contact.

Country of Origin: USA

Possibility of death or serious injury: Like taxes and misogyny, they're inevitable.

Embarrassing clothing: It depends where you buy your Y-fronts.

Greatest hazard: Usually your opponent.

Watch out for: Some of the worst tattoos known to humankind.

Prize/Rewards: The satisfaction of two months in traction, knowing that the guy you beat will be out of action for four.

People most likely to enjoy it: Sociopathic, sadistic exhibitionists.

Expect to hear: "1 - 2 - 3 - 4 -5 - 6 - 7 - 8 - 9 - 10, you're out!"

These two are just pussying around for the camera. Call that a fist...?

History

Bare-knuckle fighting is something that's been happening for as long as man has been walking upright and which people have been getting paid to do, and been paying to watch, for about three hundred years.

You'll Need...

Your two hands, and depending on the sanctioning body you're fighting under, your feet, elbows, knees, teeth, forehead and thumbs (for gouging). Different bodies allow different variations on the classic rules of bare-knuckle fighting. The classic rules state that combatants must not wear any form of either padding or armament on their fists (hence bare-knuckle) and that an opponent may not be struck while he is down, but this is a rule promoters have pretty much abandoned. UFC is the current king of the hill in terms of profile, having dropped its no-holds-barred label and filing itself under the category of Mixed Martial Arts in order to be recognised as a legitimate sport rather than a form of video nasty.

How You Do It

It's very simple. Two grown men do pretty much anything they want to hurt each other, while dressed in their Y-fronts.

Advanced

While fights will frequently start and/or end explosively, there's usually a prolonged session where opponents roll around in their underwear, limbs interlocked and grunting sweet nothings into each other's ears. While it all may look a lot like a gay porno movie, getting into one of these clinches with your opposite number is without doubt the best way to avoid leaving the ring in a body bag.

19

BASE Jumping

As extreme sports go, there are few more extreme than BASE jumping, a pastime that takes the thrill of skydiving, the buzz of lawbreaking and blends it with the rush of that extra possibility of ending up as flat as the cat in a *Tom and Jerry* cartoon.

Country of Origin: USA

Possibility of death or serious injury: Yes. Technically, BASE jumping is termed "semi-suicide".

Embarrassing clothing: No, but the concealed parachute underneath your jacket will help give the impression that hunchbacks love taking the elevator to the top floor of tall buildings. Victor Hugo was way ahead of his time.

Greatest hazard: Where do you want to start...? Fierce crosswinds can ruin your whole day, while strong updraughts have been known to keep parachutists airborne for over an hour. People who regularly say, "Doh, I'd forget my head if it wasn't screwed on," don't make very good BASE jumpers, for obvious reasons.

Watch out for: Selfish, self-obsessed people attempting to top themselves and crowding out the best locations to jump from on skyscrapers.

Prize/Rewards: The knowledge that you have stared death in the face and taunted the grim reaper. Ol' Grim don't like that over much and will be sure to try harder next time.

People most likely to enjoy it: Thrill-seekers with a lemming tendency. Lemmings themselves can't abide BASE jumpers and regard them with utter scorn as lightweights. Not that it matters too much as they'll be going over a cliff very shortly.

Expect to hear: "Live fast, die young and leave a flat-looking corpse."

Contrary to popular belief, most BASE jumpers don't have 'I Believe I Can Fly' by R. Kelly playing on their i-Pod as they leap over the edge. Or the theme from *M.A.S.H.* Or 'Zoom' by Fat Larry's Band.

History

Of all the qualities in the human psyche, arguably the most important, even more than love, is curiosity. It was curiosity that led man's fishy ancestors out of their primordial swamp and onto dry land. It was curiosity that spurred him to employ elements of the natural world to increase his own comfort. And it was curiosity that drove him to cross the oceans, to explore the extremities of our incredible world and to turn his eyes to the stars, always looking to explore and expand his understanding of the universe around him. Sadly, this same quality is the one that leads your four-year-old to wonder whether that saucepan will make them look like a transformer if they wedge it hard enough onto their head. It's the same quality that led the American voting public to wonder if George

Bush Jr. could make an even bigger arse of the job second time round. And in 1978 it led a group of adventurous idiots to ask the question, "What would happen if we tried skydiving but took the aeroplane out of the equation?"

You'll Need...

BASE is formed from Building, Antennae, Span and Earth. You'll need one of these to jump from. And a parachute. Parachutes are typically designed to be deployed at no less than 2,000 feet, at which point a skydiver will be about 11 seconds from a pressing appointment with terra firma. So the good news for first time BASE jumpers is that you won't have to go to the trouble or expense of taking a reserve 'chute – if your main one doesn't open properly you'll barely have time for a just-in-case-Richard-Dawkins-was-wrong prayer, let alone for deploying a spare. The minimum height you can get away with is reckoned to be about 150 feet – in other words – Nelson's Column.

How You Do It

The biggest challenge for most BASE jumpers is not the jumping but the gaining access to the BASEs themselves. So whether you're looking to leap from a monument like the Eiffel Tower, Paris, a corporation headquarters like the Rialto Towers, Melbourne, or a suicide hotspot like Clifton Suspension Bridge, chances are the building's tenants or trustees, plus the local health and safety executive will have something to say about it. In fact, BASE jumping philosophy tends to be not to ask permission in the first place. Many BASE jumpers will take a break from their itinerant lifestyles to take jobs on new high-rise builds that allow them access to jump points.

Advanced

Despite the apparent risks, statistics show that jumping off tall buildings, cliffs or even high bridges kills very few people...

Why You Shouldn't Bother

...landings, however, tend to be fatal. You may not have given yourself the distance to solid ground you'd achieve in a plane, but you'll still be travelling plenty fast enough to make an impressive statement on the pavement if anything goes wrong.

Jump shoes? Check. Mobile phone? Check. Wallet and I.D.? Check. Now, there was something else important I knew I had to bring...

"This horse walks into a bar..."

Baseball

Baseball is one of the few modern sports to be mentioned in a Jane Austen novel. In the classic *Northanger Abbey* the village children go off to play "base-ball"... after which they grab a KFC bargain bucket and rent a DVD.

Country of Origin: England

Possibility of death or serious injury: Only if you're a passing pigeon with no awareness of when the batter's about to connect with a pitch.

Embarrassing clothing: Not in the slightest, Sir, it's a game that has given us the most ubiquitous of headgear – the baseball cap. Just imagine if it had been different and it had been lawn bowls that had fired up the sporting interest of America for the last 100 years. Instead of Boyz-n-the-Hood hanging out on street corners with their baseball caps back to front, they'd be there with the big boombox, the flat white caps and the pressed white trousers...

Greatest hazard: Getting a knuckleball on the helmet at 65mph.

Prize/Rewards: A career that can last a lot longer than most pro athletes, especially when helped by steroids.

History

Baseball evolved from the English game of rounders, though even before it left the British Isles it was being referred to as "base ball". Celebrated English novelist Jane Austen wrote her novel *Northanger Abbey* between 1798 and 1803 and referred to the children of the village playing a game of "base-ball". In the USA they swapped the softball for the hardball and from 1845 onward the popularity of the sport grew. In England they also swapped to a hard ball for rounders and the game was taken up enthusiastically by the Girl Guide movement. The "inside game" of its early professional days, where players had to scratch for runs, was replaced by a game dominated by big hitters like Babe Ruth after World War One. A "gentleman's agreement" kept African-American players out of the game, who not surprisingly had a variety of different names for this unwritten racial bar, none of them printable here. The signing of Jackie Robinson by the Brooklyn Dodgers in 1946 marked the first signs of this agreement being abandoned, and the major league became fully integrated within a trifling quarter of a century or thereabouts. The legitimate mumblings of discontent from exploited players crystallised during the 1919 Black Sox scandal, and the players' unions have grown in power ever since, to the point where the only people getting stiffed now are the fans who are forced to miss out on doses of their favourite sport when millionaire players feel like buying another solid gold bathtub, as they did in 1972, 1981 and 1994. Baseball has become something the majority of Americans are proud to call the national sport and one they can certainly claim to dominate. In 89 years of the Baseball World Series, no team from outside the U.S. has yet to be crowned victorious. Apart from Canada.

You'll Need...

No one's too sure why everybody decided to start wearing pyjamas to play it, but a set of these from your local department store will certainly be cheaper than a trip to the USA to buy the real stuff. Don't be fooled by the logo-covered long T-shirts and caps on sale in your local high street. Like the French with their wine, only the cheap rubbish gets exported. The quality product never leaves its country of origin.

Ah, bless. This sparky youngster in Little League is carrying on the great American tradition of taking a simple sport and adding layers of statistical complexity that would give Stephen Hawking a headache.

How You Do It

Much has been made of the strategy required to win a game of baseball. In particular, baseball is lauded over the other two most popular team games in the U.S., football and basketball, because there is no element of killing the clock involved. The reality is that, like cricket, it takes so long to play the commentators have little else to do but what they're paid to do – talk. Regardless of whether they have anything of worth to say. Average game length has gone from 90 minutes at the turn of the last century to 166 minutes at the turn of this one. It's inevitable that analysts and pundits blather about the tactics behind this decision, that dropped catch or the other's appalling hair styling. From a playing perspective all you need to know is, if you're in to bat, you want to knock the ball into the stands, if you're in to pitch you want to get the batter out.

Advanced

The simplicity of the game doesn't necessarily make it any easier of course. With the turf war between pitchers and hitters over the rules currently in a state of uneasy ceasefire, the game itself boils down to the same skills we all learnt at nursery school and a lapse in ability can still cause a red face. Helpfully the American vocabulary has provided the game with two great labels for the two major classes of player. Play heroically and you'll be a "hero"; play like an idiot and you'll be a "goat".

Why You Shouldn't Bother

It's rounders, isn't it? It's as much a part of growing up as ring-o-ring-o-roses, climbing trees and getting measles. We don't have international hopscotch tournaments, so why make a big thing out of "base-ball".

The better out-fielders tend to choose positions in *front* of the batter.

Birdman Competitions

Those magnificent men in their flying machines, they don't go up at all, they just go down down down like that burning ring of fire…

Country of Origin: Greece	

Possibility of death or serious injury: Serious physical damage is rare. A propeller in the face is a typical injury, but as they are turning at half a revolution a second, survival rates are usually high.

Embarrassing clothing: …is all part of the fun. A twenty-first century version of Caractacus Potts from *Chitty Chitty Bang Bang* is about right.

Greatest hazard: Very large cats.

Prize/Rewards: Difficult to say as no one has ever "won" but there is a certain amount of kudos.

People most likely to enjoy it: Men who like to spend a lot of time in the garage. Rejects from the TV series *Scrapheap Challenge*.

Expect to hear: "For a second you really looked like you were going to make it."

of drag, thrust and lift to be able to defy gravity, the questions did not stop. To this day the debate rages over how the common bumblebee is able to stay in the air. What is undeniable is that it does – and that in understanding how it does we must take into consideration such complex effects as dynamic stall, and how the bumblebee is capable of encountering this airflow-induced vortex in every one of its oscillation cycles, for it is this which allows him, against apparently insurmountable odds, to take to the air and stay there. All of which is somewhat lost on competitors in birdman competitions, who fling themselves from the end of piers, the tops of wharf side buildings and the centre of bridges in the misguided belief that they too can beat physics and soar into the clouds like a swallow. The central paradox here is not so much, "How can a man generate sufficient air pressure differentials with only the force of his own body to produce the lift and thrust required?" as "How can this bunch of cretins spend such a vast amount of time and effort on something so utterly pointless?"

History

Ever since Icarus set off on the wrong flightpath, man has believed he has it within him to fly like the birds. The question of whether he would ever achieve this is one which has been pondered by minds as great as that of Leonardo Da Vinci, and it is one that continues to both fascinate and in many cases mystify the scientific community. Even when the Wright Brothers were finally able to create a craft capable of achieving enough power to maintain an effective ratio between the forces

You'll Need…

To find a competition. The major U.K. competition used to be held in Bognor Regis, but with the kind of long-term planning that tells you all you need to know about the U.K. tourist industry, the end of the pier was recently demolished making the landing area – that is the patch of water directly beneath the take off zone – too shallow to guarantee the competitors would be safe from serious injury. Aside from denying this seaside town one of its few major annual attractions, this has also denied a lot of innocent fun for the bloodthirsty mob who annually gather to witness the carnage, as well as being a missed opportunity for the human race as a whole to improve the gene pool.

How You Do It

Whereas old-style Birdman competitions awarded prizes solely based on distance of flight, the good news for competitors is that most contests – of which the Red Bull sponsored "Flug Tag" is the most prominent – also award points based on creativity and showmanship. This emphasis does at least mean that the organisers are a lot more transparent about what they expect from their seven entrants. It is not so much "unpowered solo flight" as "falling into water with a certain panache".

Advanced

Advertising in Red Bull Flug Tag is restricted to a single square foot. In the past, notable sponsors of these misguided crafts have been the campaign to keep Steve McClaren working in English football and the Paris Hilton appreciation society.

Why You Shouldn't Bother

In the entire history of sporting competition there remains no other event where not a single competitor has yet to achieve the stated aim of the contest. Birdman takes pointlessness to new levels.

Two metres out from the pier and this competitor is claimed by the unflinching forces of Madame Gravity. Serious beardy types with gossamer-winged hang-gliders are frowned upon, men who have rummaged around in builders' skips are what it's all about. U.K. Athletics have asked that "Making a Tit of Yourself" be considered an Olympic sport for the 2012 games in London.

Bodybuilding

You will have to shave yourself all over, wax your bum crack, and slather yourself in creosote. If you're a guy your parts will shrivel up. Ladies can wave goodbye to their breasts. You will then have to appear in public wearing little more than six inches of dental floss so that people can look at your grossly disproportioned body. And bodybuilders wonder why they don't get more respect...

Country of Origin: India

Possibility of death or serious injury: Those who are tempted by the dark path; muscle mass built on the house of sand that is pills and injections may find unwelcome side effects as the years roll by – such as your limbs seizing up.

Embarrassing clothing: No way. That bright pink thong deftly cleaving your carefully shaved, painted and oiled butt crack, and cradling testicles the size of two black olives looks totally awesome.

Greatest hazard: Being mistaken for Madonna.

Prize/Rewards: Yes, there's stuff you can win, especially big trophies. And because it's bodybuilding they award trophies that only bodybuilders can pick up.

People most likely to enjoy it: ...are to be pitied.

Expect to hear: "Man, I am so pumped up!"

History

First conceived in India, bodybuilding went worldwide in the nineteenth century after a promotional tour by a Prussian man with a moustache established a business model combining public performances and aspirational marketing with products of questionable benefit that proved hugely successful and still drives the business today.

It garnered some interest in the U.K., with the country's first bodybuilding event being held at that most famous of serious sporting venues, the Royal Albert Hall, and was judged by amongst other luminaries, Sir Arthur Conan Doyle. But the sport found its true home in America, a nation where merit is always afforded based on size and show rather than suitability for purpose, and bodybuilding has now become a multi billion-dollar industry.

You'll Need...

To love yourself above all others. You'll also need to travel a lot to the various competitions around the globe all with improbable names, such as Mr. Olympia, Mr. Universe and Mr. Muscle Beach, when more appropriate names might be: Mr. Freak, Mr. Burst Blood Vessel and Mr. Hernia.

How You Do It

Put simply, the sport of bodybuilding is the process of increasing muscle mass to extreme proportions, a process known specifically as hypertrophy. You'll need to combine a rigorously planned training and exercise regime with a carefully structured diet rich in protein and carbohydrates. Make sure that your body fat is carefully monitored and consult a qualified trainer on how you should modify your regime and diet as competition time approaches. Then a few days before performance, shoot yourself full of steroids and hit the tanning salon. Book a booth for the entire day and expose yourself to levels of radiation that would send the Incredible Hulk to

It may look like a man in an inflatable muscle suit, but no, this look can be achieved with careful exercise and good, wholesome food from mother nature's larder.

the couch with an ice pack on his head for a lie down. Now, the day before the competition, stop drinking water. Or anything else. Shoot some more drugs. Go to the competition. Apply fake tan for that too-long-on-the-barbecue look and then ponce around in fluorescent underwear. If you're female, you'll need to do all of the above, plus find time to put make-up on with a yard brush.

Advanced

Early bodybuilders based their quest for physical perfection around the proportions between shoulders, chest, waist and thighs that would correspond to the classical golden ratio of 1.618. In strictly classical terms this would put Brad Pitt, of all men on earth, at the closest approximation to the classical musculature ideal, with Madonna a close second. Contemporary competition body builders have actually abandoned the idea of

the golden ratio, partly because they're clearly more interested in developing huge scary boggle eyes and bulging neck veins, and partly because the dehydration and steroid intake prohibits them from engaging in anything as mentally challenging as calculating mathematical ratios. Or walking and talking at the same time.

Why You Shouldn't Bother

There aren't that many sports where drug taking, dehydration, implant surgery, exposure to potentially carcinogenic levels of UV rays, and sterility inducing underwear are considered essential for success. And that's before we even get started on the narcissistic complex you're likely to develop from staring at yourself in the mirror for three hours a day. Plus at the end of it all you'll look truly terrifying with your clothes off, look prematurely old, and your arteries will never forgive you.

Bog Snorkelling

There are stories of odd things seen in lonely, desolate bogs: will-o'-the-wisps, the ghosts of those who have lost their lives to the treacherous, sucking pits, and men with snorkels on a bike...

Country of Origin: Wales

Possibility of death or serious injury: It depends how unexpectedly deep the bog is. Or if there's a bog troll in residence.

Embarrassing clothing: Spend a Saturday night in Swansea city centre or a Friday night in Mumbles when the hen parties hit town and you'll soon realize that lurching about like the creature from the black lagoon with a snorkel is relatively conservative dress in Wales.

Prize/Rewards: A cold hose down and a clip round the ear from the wife when she sees the state of your whites.

People most likely to enjoy it: The kind of person that thinks underwater cave exploration is a good thing.

Potential expansion: A bigger bog, more bogs, maybe even a Tour de Wales.

Expect to hear: "Good crowd here today – they both made it."

History

The capacity to learn is seen by many anthropologists as the crucial determining factor in the advancement of the human race. Of course not all new ideas turn out to be good ones, and we can all look back and laugh at the days when we thought the earth was flat and that Sarah Ferguson would make a great Royal. But whilst there's much to be learned from making dreadful mistakes, there should also be a point at which instinct kicks in. Evidence that we are losing this ability to make a snap decision on whether something is a good or bad idea surrounds us – but nowhere is it more damning than in the smallest town in Britain – Llanwrtyd Wells – where every year the annual Bike Bog Snorkelling event is held. To the general indifference of all.

You'll Need...

A mountain bike whose tyres have been filled with a mixture of lead and water. Whilst the actual ratio of lead to water is kept a closely guarded secret, what is clear is that this unusual mix makes the bikes fairly unsuitable for using on roads, even on the lonely and unending ones of Wales.

How You Do It

The arena for competition is a trench dug into a particularly ugly part of the Waen Rhydd bog. The idea is that you cycle two lengths of the bog and record your best possible time.

Why You Shouldn't Bother

You ride a bike underwater, through a bog, in Wales. Is it so hard we have to spell it out...?

You could be the Usain Bolt of the bog snorkelling world, but who is going to care? No one. Not even your mum.

Bowls

It's often said that youth is wasted on the young so it's nice that there are some things you only get to enjoy once you've reached a certain age. Being a bit forgetful. Free public transport. Fortified wine. Being a bit forgetful. And bowls.

Country of Origin: England

Possibility of death or serious injury: Bowls is really BASE jumping for crumblies. Those spindly legs could go at any minute, and if they do, no one's walking away from a one-metre collision with a bone-hard, carefully manicured green at that age.

Embarrassing clothing: When was the last time you saw a 95-year-old wear anything else?

Greatest hazard: Forgetting to let go of the wood and being dragged down the green after it.

Prize/Rewards: A cup of tea and the weak applause of those among your fellow players whose wrists are still up to it after a strenuous game.

People most likely to enjoy it: The old. It won't make them live any longer, but it will get them out in the open air where they don't smell as bad.

Expect to hear: "Sorry dear, what were we talking about?"

Dare you enter the arena of death...?

History

The game of bowls, a sport that's as old amongst its peers in the world of sports as the people who play it are amongst the members of their heartless, uncaring communities. Famously played by Sir Francis Drake and Walter Raleigh shortly before they beat the Spanish Armada, bowls is recorded as far back as the thirteenth century and by all accounts of anyone who currently plays it was a much better game in those days. And like hearing about your gran's teenage tearaway years, you may be surprised to hear that bowls has some surprisingly edgy roots. It was banned by monarchy and parliament alike for fear that its growing popularity would lead to a decline in archery, fencing, morris dancing and other pursuits that helped hone the nation's martial skills. Nowadays of course, bowls is a game that's popular the world over, especially amongst those who favour elasticated trouser waists and Honda Civics.

You'll Need...

Bowls is played with balls that are every bit as wonky as the limbs of the wrinklies that hurl them. You'll need a set of these things, which are sometimes called "woods" in nostalgia for the days before they were made of plastic. You'll also need bowling attire. You may find it hard to tell just what it is that distinguishes traditional bowling wear – conservative slacks, deathly dull shirts, narcolepsy-inducing jumpers and oh-so-comfy shoes – from the kind of one-step-from-the-grave outfits bowling fans wear to go about their everyday business of drawing their pensions, writing complaining letters to the *Daily Mail* and generally getting in the way. But step into any good sporting wear shop and check out the price tag. You'll soon see the difference is about 20 per cent.

How You Do It

For a sport that's largely played by the elderly, the terminally uncool and the easily offended, there are a surprisingly high number of terms that are open to cheap-shot *double entendres* that are the resort of only the very lowest kind of wit. Essentially players are competing to get their big oddly shaped balls as close to the little white kitty as possible. All players are competing to get close to one kitty or sweety. Whoever gets closest is said to have scored. Ideally players will manage to leave their balls touching the kitty.   Players can achieve

different effects based on the number of fingers they grip their balls with – "finger pegging" and "backhand draw" are just a couple of the more inventive options.

Advanced

Did I mention that the small ball is also sometimes called a jack? Sometimes players will be so forceful with their balls that they'll knock the jack off. I don't know what this is called. But I bet it sounds rude.

Why You Shouldn't Bother

Unless you're already living in a twilight world and can remember what black and white television was like, bowls is a sport that you'll have plenty of time for in between retiring and dying. In fact you can combine the two. The grim reaper has been known to hang around bowls clubs waiting for business. Like a taxi on a taxi rank, 'ol Grim knows that there'll be someone heading his way in a minute. If you're already retired then frankly I'm surprised you're reading this and would like to apologise sincerely for any offence caused. Except you're probably unable to read it, or anything else written here without your glasses. No, not those ones. Your readers. Yes. You can't find them? Then I won't bother.

To the left, to the right or straight-on? The choice of trajectories in bowls is dazzling.

 **Boxing**

Head examinations are mandatory and provided for fighters after the fight. You may like to undergo one voluntarily now if you're seriously thinking about taking this sport up.

Country of Origin: Greece

Possibility of death or serious injury: If you do it often enough then you stand a good chance of detaching something vital. Basically, you're going into a ring to do what most people spend their life avoiding – physical punishment.

Embarrassing clothing: Only, it seems, if you're Chris Eubank.

Watch out for: His "sweet" right jab. Oooof, no, you missed it.

Prize/Rewards: With the great big belts given to champions you can be sure your trousers will never fall down again.

People most likely to enjoy it: Anyone with an IQ that is close to their shoe size, or who has a penchant for sado-masochism.

Expect to hear: The bell, after what seems like half an hour.

History

The history of boxing is one that goes back as far as the dawn of time. The ancient Greeks drew up a list of rules for the sport they called pugilism, which forbade opponents from holding, hugging or kissing each other until the bout was over, and gave each fighter strips of leather to wear and protect their knuckles. Then about 3,000 years later the Marquess of Queensberry endorsed a set of 12 rules, the most notable being the use of big padded gloves which allowed each fighter to take a pounding for a lot longer, and the sport of boxing as we know it today was brought blood-soaked, bewildered and bawling into the world.

You'll Need...

Humble origins. If one too many disappointing pay-per-view events and a couple of boxercise classes have convinced you that you've got what it takes to make it as a fighter, then it might be a good idea to take yourself down to a gym that doesn't have time-release air fresheners for a taste of what you can expect. The majority of fighters come from poor backgrounds with limited access to good education or employment. Ultimately, even the most successful boxers are at risk of permanent disability and/or disfigurement. And not just from the legion of personal advisers who convince them that a Maori style tattoo across the side of their face is just what they need to get their career back on track.

How You Do It

You hit your opponent a lot while deftly dodging the blows they aim at you. In reality you get hit a lot until they stretcher you away in a heap.

Advanced

There are several defined styles of boxing from the classic out-fighting style which prizes jab technique and controlling the fight over power, to an in-fighting style reliant on maintaining proximity and throwing hook and uppercut combinations. Until you have determined what style suits you the main thing to bear in mind is to protect your head. Your head contains your brain. It also houses your eyes, ears, mouth and nose. So as body parts go, it's fairly important and you need to remember at all times that if your opponent is hitting you in the head it may severely impair your ability to enjoy the rest of your life.

Bullfighting

The Spanish have long been masters of creating sports out of animal cruelty and after establishing various fiestas where donkeys were abused, they came up with the pinnacle of their achievements – bullfighting.

Country of Origin: Spain

Possibility of death or serious injury: High, but not high enough. As a rule of thumb you should avoid any sport where the word "gored" is used frequently.

Embarrassing clothing: As a matador you'll be expected to wear the kind of metrosexual outfit even David Beckham might find a little showy, comprising ballet pumps, sequined pedal pushers, a natty little jacket that doesn't quite fit and a Mickey Mouse hat. You certainly wouldn't wear that kind of gear round Brisbane city centre of a Friday night without risk of being dumped into a catering bin.

Greatest hazard: Getting the horn.

Prize/Rewards: The usual: money, fame, adoring women throwing themselves at your feet with a rose between their teeth.

People most likely to enjoy it: Narrow-hipped, high-buttocked narcissists. Every Spanish waiter, in fact.

Expect to hear: "Ole!"

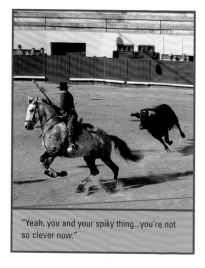

"Yeah, you and your spiky thing...you're not so clever now."

quietly made their excuses and ushered themselves out of the public eye, bullfighting remains a big deal in Spain and South America, as well as being immortalized in the literature of Ernest Hemingway, the paintings of Edouard Manet, and videos for instantly forgettable Madonna album fillers.

You'll Need...

At least one bull, although each matador will usually face two, both of whom will make guest appearances on local tapas menus later that night, sometimes sharing the bill with any horses unlucky enough not to make it through the day's proceedings. You'll also need a full entourage of assistants – two picadors (lancers), three bandilleros (flagmen) and a mozo de espadas (sword page), who has the most important job, as he'll be responsible for taking care of your outfit and ensuring that you don't experience any wardrobe malfunctions.

History

Many see bullfighting as little more than savagery, a celebration of barbarism that should not be tolerated in any part of the civilised world, or even Spain. Bullfighting is certainly a sport in the great historic tradition of those where a certain amount of suffering is not so much an unfortunate but unavoidable by-product as an essential part of the fun. But whereas bear baiting and cock fighting have

Plans to even things out a bit by equipping the bulls with a team of highly trained Jack Russells have so far met stiff resistance both from the Matador's Union and the Association of Jack Russell Owners.

How You Do It

Stage one of the ritualized slaughter sees the bull being tested for its ferocity by the matador, who'll be wearing his lovely magenta and gold cape. Just in case the bull isn't feeling ferocious, one of the helpful picadors is on hand. From the relative safety of (armoured) horseback he'll draw first blood with a well aimed jab to the neck. Stage two gets the three amigos, sorry, bandilleros, in on the fun. They'll aim to plant their razor-sharp barbed sticks in as close to the original wound as possible to ensure maximum blood loss. Finally, after more costume changes than a Kylie concert, the matador does a bit of fancy twirling with his little red cape in front of the mortally wounded bull before putting the thing out of its misery with a sword through the heart.

Advanced

In exceptional cases, when the bull has fought particularly bravely, the President of the Plaza can grant a bull "indulto", which is considered a great honour for the bull. In these rare cases the bull will be spared a humiliating death in the ring and led out to bleed to death in private.

Why You Shouldn't Bother

Despite modern innovations and safety regulations introduced in the twentieth century, bullfighting remains extremely dangerous, especially for bulls. Many modern variations on the traditional format have emphasised the clowning elements of the contest, and some have gone so far as to do away with the violent death of the bull. But like fat-free yoghurt, thongs for men and modern Woody Allen films, these have proved universally unpopular.

No, love, you're right. That purple just doesn't go with the blue.

Bungee Jumping

Not to be recommended for those with prosthetic legs, bungee jumping is the craze that swept the world a decade ago, which means those big elastic bands are getting a little bit old now...

Country of Origin: England

Possibility of death or serious injury: Surprisingly low, but statistics like these are just aching to change.

Embarrassing clothing: Strapless tops are not advisable for women as the forces of gravity tend to exceed the restraining power of lycra and M&S fasteners.

Watch out for: Burst blood vessels in the eye giving the jumper a rather fetching "demon" appearance for the next four to six weeks.

Prize/Rewards: You'll be considerably out of pocket, but will have gained valuable insight into just why the fear of heights is such a popular phobia.

People most likely to enjoy it: Depressives who want to dip their toe in the water before eating the whole enchilada.

Expect to hear: "Is it too late for me to change my mi..."

History

Bungee jumping owes its ancient roots to the crazy youths of the South Pacific island of Vanuatu who threw themselves from treetops with their feet attached to vines in a test of courage that bears a striking resemblance – and a similar level of idiocy – to those modern youths who surf elevators, suburban commuter trains and slow-moving lorries. The first modern bungee jumps took place in the English city of Bristol, from the local community's suicide-spot-of-choice, the Clifton Suspension Bridge. The jumpers from Oxford University's Dangerous Sports Club were arrested immediately afterwards, presumably by a pair of coppers who were glad to be able to make an arrest rather than getting out another body bag. A few years later the Kiwis started taking jumps off the Kawarau Bridge on the South Island and started claiming the idea as their own. And the fact that they did establish the first commercial site for doing it probably makes them as close to the creators as anyone.

The difficult bit was five seconds ago.

You'll Need…

To have taken leave of your senses, or have agreed to undertake a jump for charity and be too much of a wimp to back out. Which almost certainly makes you way too much of a wimp for what you're about to do. Most professional jump organisers will provide you with a bungee cord, harness and everything you need for your jump.

How You Do It

The good news for anyone still committed to briefly experiencing the working life of a yo-yo is that once you've jumped, there really is nothing to it. The bad news is that making yourself jump may well be one of the least pleasant things you ever have to do. There's a reason for this. Jumping off ledges to our certain death is something we've evolved to realise is not good for us. We may well all have been fascinated enough by the drop to wonder what it would be like to jump, but for the vast majority of us that's as far as it goes.

Jumpers can choose an option to wash'n'go.

Why You Shouldn't Bother

For 20 seconds of terror/excitement, there's weeks of nervous anxiety, plus ten minutes of dangling like a fat worm on a fishing line while the blood rushes to your head.

Where it all started on a commercial basis, the Kawarau Bridge near Queenstown, NZ. These days you can buy a T-shirt of your jump, a photo, a DVD, a model of the bridge, plus fresh underwear.

Buzkashi

It's just like polo, but instead of a bunch of Hooray Henrys lumping a ball round a manicured field, gritty Afghan tribesmen compete for a goat carcass. So, a few differences, but lots of similarities.

Country of Origin: Afghanistan

Possibility of death or serious injury: Not a great deal higher than any other activity in Afghanistan. Unless you're a goat.

Embarrassing clothing: No, unless you're particularly fussy about getting goat-blood spatters on your cardy.

Greatest hazard: The goat becoming entangled in your moustache.

Prize/Rewards: It's trampled goat on toast for the winners and a consolation landmine for the losers. Unlike soccer, if you score a hat-trick you don't get to keep the goat after the game.

People most likely to enjoy it: Hard-bitten mountain men who haven't had the opportunity to experience a no-holds-barred game of Buckaroo.

Potential expansion: With many of the senior players reaching retirement age there is a fear that many Buzkashi skills will be lost, and so NATO troops are helping set up a Buzkashi Little League where teenagers play with a headless Himalayan badger.

Expect to hear: "I have scored a goat!"; "Do you know what really gets my goat, Hamed?"; "That was a goat out of nowhere"; and "You missed an open goat!"

History

For such a remote and seemingly insignificant part of the world, the country of Afghanistan has given the world a great deal. Nice rugs, the supermodels of the canine world, and of course approximately half the planet's heroin. Most notably in the last couple of centuries Afghanistan has dished out approximately 99 different kinds of hell to any outside influences who've tried to get involved in shaping its future, from the British in the 1840s, to the Russians in the 1980s, and full circle to the International Force spearheaded by the Americans and errr, British, again, right now. What with all the rug making, hound grooming, poppy harvesting and CIA-sponsored guerrilla warfare training, it's no wonder that in the last few decades the busy Afghans haven't always been able to find the time in their packed schedules for sporting activities. So when they do it's not surprising that their most famous sport is one that combines their tough image with their superior equine skills and their more general love of animals. Animals that aren't goats, anyway.

You'll Need...

Friends with horses and lots of time on their hands. And lots of them too. Also a goat. But not any old goat – a nicely balanced and springy goat is best. Behead it, disembowel it, and place the carcass in a large vat full of water to soak overnight. You might want to add a little splash of balsamic vinegar. As far as clothes go, you can wear anything you like except goat Velcro which was banned in 2002.

How You Do It

Anyone who's seen the last *Rambo* movie will be familiar with how this crazy sport is played, albeit only because that's what happens in the opening 10 minutes before you had the chance to drift off into the sweet release of sleep. Riders compete to capture the carcass from a goal in the centre of the playing area and transport it around a distant pole before returning it to claim a point. Rules wise, pretty much anything goes, and the whips carried by the riders aren't solely for use on their mounts. There are many phrases that have sprung up around Buzkashi. If you accidentally drop the goat at the wrong point, then that is called an "own-goat". A rider who manages to thwart another rider at the last second is said to have made a "goat line clearance". If scores are tied at the end of the game, the contest is decided by the first person to score a "golden goat".

Advanced

Afghans prize a good horse, and many of Buzkashi's most successful players are men in their forties and fifties who've had the chance not merely to learn the skills required of the game, but have also developed excellent understanding of the horses in their stables and how best to train them. This makes Buzkashi one of the least ageist sports on the planet, so if you're in the throes of a mid-life crisis but can't afford a Ferrari and look absurd in Speedos this might just be the thing for you.

Why You Shouldn't Bother

If you are not born an Afghan, then you can only play in one of the lesser positions, such as 6th Hoof or Pole Defence. There is an intense fear that the Americans will bring not only democracy to the country, but also sports statistics and that Afghan punters will have to memorise goat strike averages. However, only in a land where the one certainty right now is that if a Taliban bomb doesn't get you, a NATO one probably will, would dragging a headless goat around while riding a galloping horse be considered light relief.

International Buzkashi player of the year Mustafa Foreleg attempts to wrestle the goat from an opposing player. Mustafa is the Cristiano Ronaldo of the Buzkashi world with a string of endorsements from leading goat butchers and moustache grooming aid suppliers.

Camel Wrestling

If you're the kind of freak who likes to watch two animals trying to tear each other to pieces, then be warned; camels fighting is to violence what two snails mating is to porn.

Country of Origin: Turkey

Possibility of death or serious injury: Only if you're wearing Eau de Camel on Heat and are dressed as the back end of a pantomime camel.

Greatest hazard: There's not a great deal of risk involved in the actual fight, but watch what you say or you could find you've swapped your wife for the winner.

Watch out for: Pints of spit.

Prize/Rewards: It's not quite up there with training the winner of the Melbourne Cup.

People most likely to enjoy it: If you think you're the kind of person who might like watching two large heaps of smelly, moth-eaten carpet banging aimlessly together, this could very well be the sport for you.

Expect to hear: "One hump or two?"

History

Whether acting as a ship of the desert, going without water for three months or carrying wise men, the camel has always played a very special role in the global culture, particularly in its native habitat of Arabia. While the commercial development of Western Europe and the Americas was largely dependent on the hard work of the horse, and the meat and produce of the cow, the nation states of what is now the Middle East have relied on the camel to do all the work of a horse with the promise that when they get too old to continue humping stuff across endless desert they can look forward to the kind of retirement enjoyed by the average head of cattle, namely being marinated and stuffed on the end of a shish kebab. And whilst the camel has retained its place as an important status symbol in Arabian culture, modern transportation methods have made it less essential in a commercial role in the regions it once dominated. So it's nice to know that there are still places that the modern camel-about-town can find gainful employment outside of appearing in zoos and advertising cigarettes. Yes, on the busy Turkish Camel Wrestling circuit.

You'll Need...

To organise your own camel wrestling bout you'll need three camels – two bull males, and one seductive young female, preferably one that's on heat. The presence of the female is essential – without her the two males will simply lounge around the place amiably, generally enjoying each other's company, scratching and breaking wind every so often. Even with the female present there's still some cajoling to be done if you don't want all three camels to simply sit down and talk things out, and possibly explore alternative relationship options in an open, caring and honest way, making sure they are clear about setting boundaries and have each other's respect and consent at every stage of the discussion.

How You Do It

Turkey is a country with a strong reputation for being a nation of animal lovers. But leaving to one side for the moment the goatherd's maxim of "what happens in the mountains stays in the mountains" many tourists are surprised to discover that such a seemingly barbaric sport is still practised today. Camel wrestling may be more authentic than WWF, but it certainly has a lot less to offer as a spectacle. For all their remarkable talents, camels make for pretty rubbish wrestlers. Expect to see signature moves such as "power neckrubbing", "extreme kneeling down, not doing much" and "piledriver trying to make a run for it", a move which can actually prove extremely dangerous for members of the audience who happen to get in the way.

Advanced

In keeping with the cultural respect accorded to them, the fighting camels are treated like royalty. They are given a parade 24 hours before the fight, a poem of tribute immediately before the bout and a prize – a rug – afterwards if they win. Sadly they are not given the opportunity to relax on their rug with the lady camel that kicked off all the trouble in the first place.

Why You Shouldn't Bother

Understandably, the camels get excited by all the pomp they're afforded, not to mention the prospect of a punch-up and/or a nifty spot of romance. As a result there are camel bodily fluids all over the place. If that isn't enough to put you off, then the prospect of being forced to move to Turkey and spending a lot of time with the Hulk Hogan of the camel world may be what tips the balance.

LIVE! from Istanbul Field, Ibrahim Ibrahim presents Turkish Camel Wrestling Federation's "Super Camel Smackdown Sunday". Watch out for the sneaky penis bite in Round 7.

Cheese Rolling

The annual cheese rolling competition takes place at Cooper's Hill near Gloucester every spring bank holiday Monday. A large Double Gloucester cheese is rolled down a very steep Cotswold slope and competitors chase after it like it was the last golden ticket in *Charlie and the Chocolate Factory*.

Country of Origin: England

Possibility of death or serious injury: Yes – broken arms, legs, wrists, collar bones.

Embarrassing clothing: No, unless you like dressing in a smock.

Greatest hazard: Slippery grass and being rolled on by another competitor. Injuries from cheese impacts are virtually unheard of.

Is it expensive? Absolutely free.

Watch out for: Cow pats.

Prize/Rewards: A cheese (Double Gloucester).

People most likely to enjoy it: Wallace and Gromit, freeloading vegetarians.

Potential expansion to: France with a *Camembert Roulant*.

Expect to hear: "I'm hoping for a slow cheese, this year."

History

No one seems to be sure why the residents of a small town outside Gloucester gather at Cooper's Hill every May to chase a cheese they roll down it. And since this inexplicable event guarantees validation in the form of a brief feature on the regional TV news every year, no one from Gloucestershire has ever wanted to question it. However, at the heart of this kind of acceptance of nonsensical behaviour lies the very essence of what it is to be English. To be English is to be accepting of the differences of others. It is to be – to a lesser or greater degree – certifiably insane. Above all it is the belief that some things are done out of a sense of tradition, and that should you happen to break an ankle and lose your job because you were chasing a wheel of Double Gloucester down a muddy hillside somewhere in the Cotswolds, then that's just what your father and your grandfather before him would have done. And his father before him too.

You'll Need...

An almost pathological penchant for Double Gloucester; of which there will be four up for grabs on the day.

How You Do It

To call this cheese rolling is about as deceptive as calling greyhound racing, electric hare hunting, since the dairy product daredevils have about as much chance of catching their quarry as Posh Spice does of actually breaking into a genuine smile any time this century. The cheese has a one-second head start on a slope that while not being particularly long is certainly steep – 1:1 in places. So it's no surprise to hear that in the past the cheese has clocked up speeds in excess of 70mph, and also frequently causes actual bodily harm to hapless spectators at the bottom.

Advanced

The Cheese Rollers is a nearby alehouse that's particularly popular with entrants. Though the fact that it's three miles' walk from Cooper's Hill probably gives them too much mulling time over their decision to throw themselves down a crusty-cow-pat grass slide, while being tumbled over with all the dignity of a pair of daggy underpants in the laundromat. Still, this

Air Vice Marshal Sir Peter Wyndham-Smythe about to launch the cheese in 1947. A kindly, if slightly simple, local points out which direction is downhill. In austere post-war Britain, this was the nation's equivalent of the opening to the Beijing Olympics.

is where many of them go to mentally prepare for the trial ahead and share tactics, which, based on the outcome of most races, rarely seem to include the radical notion of trying to stay out of hospital for a change.

Why You Shouldn't Bother

There are plenty of acceptable reasons for ending up in the accident and emergency department. Being attacked by your neighbourhood gang of knife-wielding hoodies, getting thumped on the bus for playing R'n'B through the speakerphone of your mobile, being knocked over by a cyclist who mounted the pavement because he'd had enough of sharing the road with inconsiderate drivers... But chasing a cheese down a hill has never been one of them. And it never will be.

Shockingly, the cheese escapes yet again. That makes it 340-0 to the cheese.

Chessboxing

The fact that high-performing brains are very rarely to be found within heads that take a brutal pounding is one reason why the sport remains such a minority interest, the other reason being its total weirdness.

Country of Origin: Netherlands

Possibility of death or serious injury: As with any physical contact/mental prowess competition, tempers can fray and there's always the possibility that you could end up in hospital having a black queen removed from somewhere unfamiliar.

Embarrassing clothing: If chessboxing teaches you one thing it's never, ever wear satin shorts with a tweed jacket.

Watch out for: Kasparov pumped up on steroids.

People most likely to enjoy it: Imagine a Venn diagram intersection of Chess Club members and Fight Club members.

Potential expansion: There is currently sponsor interest in WWF Snooker.

Expect to hear: "I want a good clean fight, no holding, no butting and no changing a move once you let go of the piece."

You'll Need…

The sharp brain, observational awareness and expert ability to think several moves ahead that are the hallmarks of any half decent chess player. Combined with the brute upper body strength, high level of aerobic fitness and pre-flattened facial features of a boxer.

How You Do It

Rounds alternate between the two disciplines, starting with chess, which at four minutes a round is afforded double the time given to the two-minute rounds of pugilism. Victory is awarded by knockout, checkmate, or judge's decision. And since it's speed chess that's being played this isn't something you can enter into with an ability to use your fists and then sleep during the chess rounds, as referees will issue warnings to any contestant who doesn't make a move. While the pool of contestants may be relatively small, the diverse skills required by this strange hybrid means that you're likely to spend each bout being either physically or mentally humiliated by your opponent.

History

When Lord Byron wasn't busy fighting duels, smoking opium or catching syphilis, he wrote the odd poem or two. In fact, he wrote a lot of odd poems. Though it was never completed, *Don Juan* did leave us with at least one line of such breathtaking prescience, namely that truth really is stranger than fiction. An apt saying for this sport. One promotor took the idle mental wanderings of a French graphic novelist and transformed chess boxing – an invention intended as a metaphor for something or other – into an actual sport.

That's a tasty looking rook to king's bishop seven, from the young contender.

Cricket

There are some aspects of English life that would make anyone with any sense wish that Germany had won the last war, among them a total inability to make a train arrive on time, dreadful sausages and cricket.

Country of Origin: England

Possibility of death or serious injury: Only if you go into bat against Brett Lee without taking the precaution of wearing a helmet, thigh pad, arm pad, cricket gloves and a box.

Embarrassing clothing: Fans at Test matches specialise in wearing it to amuse each other, because it's the only guarantee of entertainment they'll have all day.

Watch out for: Streakers.

Prize/Rewards: A greater understanding of the weather.

People most likely to enjoy it: The comatose. They can be wakened at any time and told, "you've missed nothing".

Expect to hear: "Amazing how he managed to disguise his googly."

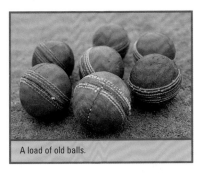

A load of old balls.

History

It takes a special talent to produce a sport that two teams can play all week only to end in a draw. One with rules so archaic and impenetrable that it takes those bits of the world that can be bothered to try learning it a couple of hundred years even to get the basics right. And who then promptly start routinely crucifying the country that invented it every time they play them. But that's the English for you. And the history of the English and the history of cricket share an awful lot of DNA.

You'll Need...

A lot of time. Just to follow the sport passively you'll need to kiss goodbye to huge chunks of your life while you listen to Test match commentators' thrilling commentary on another dreary performance by England or the consistency of the Battenberg cake they've just been served with afternoon tea. The game's inexplicable popularity in such disparate parts of the planet means that throughout the year there'll be a big game available to view on TV, usually at an unearthly hour of the night. Should you be foolish enough to actually want to play the game at amateur level you'll need to set aside half your weekend. That time you'll spend making soggy cucumber sandwiches and ensuring your whites are suitably pristine. The other half of the weekend you'll spend playing, and during this time you can expect at least a couple of minutes actual sporting activity. Assuming it doesn't rain – which, if you're playing in the U.K., it will.

How You Do It

Each team has 11 players, a couple of whom will possess a degree of talent for hitting, throwing and catching, and one of whom will actually understand the rules. The two umpires are responsible for holding everyone's jumper and counting to six. The talented players will

An idyllic English view, ruined by cricket.

take turns hitting, throwing and catching the red leather ball. Everyone else will stand around looking vaguely attentive. Sometimes people feel motivated to move a big white panel called a sidescreen. Nobody knows why, because it makes no difference. Very occasionally a sequence of play will involve the ball being both thrown and hit. There may even be some catching involved too. In these extremely rare instances any assembled spectators will mark the occasion with a smattering of applause, before drifting off to the crossword or sudoku again. The whole process grinds on until it gets dark or starts raining, whichever comes first.

Advanced

Cricket has had the reputation for being a gentleman's game since the long lost days of the British Empire. Stretching back to the time of W.G. Grace, it has a history that is littered with tales of match fixing, bodyline bowling and racial abuse, along with players indulging in wild tour incidents involving drink, drugs, groupies and unauthorised use of pedaloes. The fact that sledging, time-wasting and ball

tampering are all accepted tactics within the game, makes it clear that the qualities that amount to being a gentleman have changed little from the days when Britain was able to paint a third of the globe red.

Why You Shouldn't Bother

While cricket exerts a vice-like hold on its traditional core audience, the fact is that they are all inching towards Alzheimer's. With a new MTV generation in mind, cricket's international governing body has been busy devising new ways of packaging their product; the most recent innovation being 20x20, which takes all the tedium and crushing sense of ennui that comes with Test cricket and condensing it into a more digestible package that can be over and done with in a mere four hours or so. This has proved remarkably popular with younger audiences and exponents of the virtues of power napping. But on the whole you're probably better off heading to Estonia. Here the game is played on ice, adding a light-hearted angle that frankly the po-faced version of the game we're all forced to sit through could really do with.

Croquet

Croquet is not as genteel as it looks. Under the mannered etiquette of the game lie dark forces waiting to be unleashed...waiting to send your ball into the depths of Hampshire.

Country of Origin: England

Possibility of death or serious injury: Only if you slip into a parallel dimension and end up playing with Alice in Wonderland.

Embarrassing clothing: Loose summer frocks with a bonnet and parasol are *de rigueur*. For women the dress code is much less formal.

Greatest hazard: A loose mallet head.

Watch out for: Moles.

People most likely to enjoy it: Social climbers and other oddballs.

Potential expansion: Currently not considered to be a great threat to soccer as the world's favourite sport.

Don't expect: Croquet chants, mallet rage, players slamming their balls into the turf, mallet abuse.

History

Croquet is a seemingly genteel and civilised sport but it's actually pretty vicious once you break it down.

You'll Need...

A grass arena the size of a village square, 12 hoops or wickets, mallets and balls for every player and a posh person to explain the rules.

How You Do It

The object of croquet in its standard form is to take your balls on a journey round the lawn that encompasses taking in all the hoops. However, most players will forgo the opportunity to advance their own game whenever they have a chance to commit acts of sabotage on their opponent's balls, which is where croquet gets its reputation for being played by snides, scum and guttersnipes. Strategically speaking, making life difficult for your opponent may not always be as advantageous for you in scoring points. But, just like office politics, there's a lot more fun playing the "dirty short-term game" than adopting a virtuous long-term plan.

Advanced

If the regular version of croquet isn't quite odd enough for you, you might like to try one of the many variations on the traditional game. Oddest of these is without doubt mondo croquet, which has its World Championships every summer in Portland, Oregon. The game is played with sledge hammers and bowling balls by competitors wearing Mad Hatter costumes. Seriously.

Why You Shouldn't Bother

Former Deputy Prime Minister John "two Jags" Prescott enjoys a game, adding all the glamour and lustre that brings.

Croquet is a bit like lawn snooker, you can hide your ball behind the black, but there's no chance for a deep screw against the cushion.

Darts

Good "arrers" is all about grouping, mental agility and nerves of steel. Though by all appearances, being a hopeless, lager-sodden, chain-smoking, pie muncher who is fat enough to influence local tides helps. And there aren't many sports that can say that.

Country of Origin: England

Possibility of death or serious injury: The mixture of alcohol and sharp, pointy things is a recipe for accidents. However, it's the accompanying darts lifestyle that is most likely to get you – the lager, the crisps, the lack of fresh air and a predilection for cholesterol.

Embarrassing clothing: Not so much the clothing and more the body that is generously poured into it.

Greatest hazard: A slippery oche.

Watch out for: Short-sighted/legless pub patrons making their way to the lavatories.

Prize/Rewards: Cash prizes along with the love and adoration of thousands of darts fans. But what is a darts fan? Imagine a motorway service station where they filtered out all the quiet people, the thin people, the middle-class people, the non-smoking people and those without a tattoo. What you'd have left is a darts audience.

People most likely to enjoy it: If lifting pints, crisps and cigarettes aren't fulfilling your right arm's exercise needs and masturbation hasn't helped, then darts might be the sport for you.

Expect to hear: "Same again please. Oh, and a packet of pork scratchings."

These are clearly not pub darts as they are all the same.

their recent military success, they might have chosen to celebrate their skills with an impromptu, mead-fuelled contest played on the exposed circular trunk cross-section of a felled tree, using a whole bunch of otherwise useless broken arrow heads. They may have been joined by Flemish mercenary archers who named the line in the ground that indicated where the players needed to stand, calling it an "oche" meaning notch. Alternatively, the name for their throwing position may have come from them deciding to stand within spitting ("hocken") distance of their target. We could speculate for hours, but ultimately the origins of this sport remain shrouded in mystery. However, what is even more of a mystery is how such a spirit-crushingly dull sport has become so popular, firstly in the United Kingdom and then increasingly around the world.

History

Darts may well have been invented by archers on their way back from Agincourt. Flushed with

You'll Need...

Beer money. While the gastro-fixation of the traditional British boozer has meant that it's now easier to find a dartboard in the theme bars of Manhattan than in a typical London local, you should still be able to find a pub that'll provide a board along with a rudimentary selection of mismatched and half-broken arrows in return for your custom. Your best bet in the U.K. is to head to the less affluent part of town. Despite being seen as a sport played by the working class, most amateur players of the game won't have done a day's work in years, being either terminally unemployed or students. Once you've found a suitable hostelry there's nothing else you'll need, although trousers with elasticated waistbands seem to be a popular choice among most professional players of the game.

How You Do It

Competitions became standardised in the 1920s and are played with three darts, the object being to be the first player to reach a total of (exactly) 501 points. This element of the game reveals one of the more surprising qualities of the world's top players, namely a facility for quick mental arithmetic that would put a NASA scientist to shame. Players are required to finish on a double, which by the time you've been playing for a few hours – at a rate of 1.75 pints an hour – could prove to be something of a challenge.

Advanced

Once you've got bored of the standard game of 501 or lost the ability to count, let alone add or subtract, you might want to move on to one of the many popular variations on the classic game. "Killer" is played by seeing who can protect their allocated number on the board for longest. "Around the Clock" sees players race to be the first to hit every number on the board in sequence. And assuming the rate of alcohol consumption remains constant then "Last Man Standing" should pretty much speak for itself.

Why You Shouldn't Bother

Unless you're looking to build the kind of physique needed for working at your local video store, the world of darts is something you should limit your contact with. It's not going to help ease your way up the greasy career pole the way that golf might – "Henderson, how about a round of darts some time...?"

The majesty of the dart in flight.

Diving

High board divers need a rare combination of steely nerve, gymnastic agility and swimming gear that leaves little to the imagination.

Country of Origin: Mexico

Possibility of death or serious injury: A belly flop from the high board can kill. Hitting your head on the diving board is to be avoided.

Embarrassing clothing: Only if you have particularly small or misshapen private parts.

Watch out for: Old women drifting out of the swimming lanes. Pedaloes. In big diving competitions keep an eye out for pervy TV cameramen who will follow you into the shower area to watch you rinse off after your dive, then lingering as you dab yourself dry, then following you into the changing room and tailing your car on the way home.

Prize/Rewards: Olympic medals, and if you're Chinese and a megahunk or megababe, big sponsorship deals and virtually your own province to run. Plus the certain knowledge that no one else looks as good in a pair of Speedos.

People most likely to enjoy it: Diving appeals to narcissists. If you're comfortable with embracing it on those grounds you're probably your own best friend already and nothing anyone might say is likely to stop you.

Expect to hear: *Sperrrlasssssh* – "Oh, and that's a shocker."

History

The act of diving is thought to have been invented soon after the invention of swimming. When man first realised that he could survive in water it didn't take him long to learn how to jump, bomb, dive and then to give up diving and build slides, mini-flumes and water parks.

You'll Need…

On the plus side, diving requires a minimum of expenditure on equipment. Swimwear is required by most civilised societies but you'll be okay without it out in the wilds – or in Scandinavia. The lack of kit is certainly appropriate for a sport that is over in the time it takes a human body to fall off the top of a house, albeit in a graceful manner with two and a half tucks, a twist and a ripple-less entry.

How You Do It

The particular challenge of diving comes from the fact that divers are judged based on what they do once they've left the board, despite the fact that by the time they've left the board there's bugger all they can do by way of controlling or changing their descent, gravity tending to have its own plans for them. For the spectators it's all over in the time it takes to blink, so the experience of watching a competition is a lot like eating a sack of marshmallows – snatched moments of exquisite sweetness but ultimately unsatisfying. Probably the most unique thing about diving is its remarkable scoring system, whereby divers are awarded points based on the difficulty of the dive that they are attempting. So a simple dive executed well can potentially be outscored by a technically complex dive that goes horribly wrong. Try this in your own life and see how far you get – "I know it looks a bit messy, but that's because I prepared the whole meal with just my elbows" or "Sorry you don't like the report boss, but you should take into account I completed it without using any letters or numbers…"

The various board heights are: **** scary, ******** **** scary, absolutely ********
****scary and totally, totally bricking it.

Advanced

Of course for most people diving is not something that's done before a panel of snotty judges but a fun recreational activity that can be done anywhere that there's a pool of water of uncharted depth. The most extreme form of this is to be found on the rocky coasts of South America, considered by many to be where the sport's most extreme form – cliff diving – was invented. Despite its hazardous image, cliff diving actually has a relatively low accident rate. The simple reason for this is that cliff divers, like Russian roulette aficionados or children's television presenters, only really ever get the chance to make one mistake. Ever.

Why You Shouldn't Bother

It's worth bearing in mind that no matter how straightforward it looks, it's always about ten times higher once you get up there. And it's a hundred times better to be the nobody who stays in the water than the somebody everyone remembers because he bottled it and had to climb down, wetting his pants on the way.

Mind your head as you go down, love.

Drag Racing

Not a bunch of transvestites chasing a really nice wig, but almost as fast and dangerous. If you're the sort of person who thrills to see a fellow human being toasted alive then you could do worse than getting involved in drag racing

Country of Origin: USA

Possibility of death or serious injury: Both. But usually death.

Embarrassing clothing: Three layers of Nomex fireproof material may not be the kind of thing that excites the readers of *GQ* magazine, but when the choice is between surviving or getting treated like a forgotten sausage on the barbecue, most drag racers decide that the bulky suit wins every time.

Greatest hazard: Meeting an agonising, fiery, high-speed demise.

Watch out for: Your parachute not opening. Otherwise you'll be phoning your pick-up crew from the next state.

Prize/Rewards: Big cash payouts and the chance to sleep with bubble-permed girls in thongs and stilettos with brains the size of walnuts, all of whom are called Charlene.

People most likely to enjoy it: Thrill-seeking redneck petrolheads. Engineers.

Potential expansion: Limited appeal outside the USA, possibly due to the availability of girls called Charlene.

Expect to hear: "Burn rubber, dude!"

Don't expect to hear: "Burn baby, burn!"

Model-T Fords rolled off the production line. The first street racers quickly realised that a conventional city block offered a simple way to mark out the race distance and would race the quarter of a mile or so with their foot flat down on the accelerator, their engines pushed to the absolute limits. Since the time it took for these early racers to complete the distance was slightly greater than if they'd got out and walked, these competitions were tolerated, but as the power and design of automobile engines grew and the risk to life and limb with it, so the illegal street racing community were forced to go further out. Meanwhile, street racing's more respectable brother, drag racing, has become a hugely marketed and respected sport that's popular wherever there's a market for big cars

Seventies discotheques have heavily influenced startline design.

History

The history of drag racing is irretrievably intertwined with that of illegal street racing, which began about an hour after the first two

Drag racing: All the thrust of a Saturn V rocket controlled with the front wheels of a supermarket trolley.

with outrageous paintjobs and a girl in a bikini leaning on the bonnet.

You'll Need…

The most incredible car/bike anyone has ever laid eyes on. Whatever the shape, it'll have big fat rear tyres and tiny, skinny front tyres. As far as extras go this is the sport that has it all. Turbochargers harness the energy of your engine's exhaust, superchargers compress air into the engine to allow greater fuel burn and power, and nitrous oxide gives you the ability to speak in a funny high-pitched voice. You'll also need a Christmas tree to start the race with, even if it's April.

How You Do It

Since races are over in seconds the key to successful drag racing is reducing reaction time. One of the most popular forms of the sport is Bracket Racing, in which drivers "dial in" their projected time to complete the course and then aim to match it in contest. This allows cars of different classes to compete on a more level playing field and makes it less about spending lots of money on dual plug heads,

intake snorkels and felange sunnermeisters, and puts more emphasis on consistency of driver performance. So, despite the fact that drag racing has a rock 'n' roll image you should try to be in bed by ten the night before.

Advanced

With more class criteria than marine biology there's bound to be a category for you, whatever hunk of junk you're driving. Always remember to spray water on your tyres just before the start of the race, and then burn it off before entering the staging phase. This may or may not increase your tyres' traction, but either way it makes the sport look a lot more exciting than it really is.

Why You Shouldn't Bother

As a sport, drag racing is a lot like celebrity spotting at a premiere. A lengthy wait for something to happen is followed by a brief period of anticipation until the stars of the show arrive, only to disappear a few seconds later. That's with the exception of Tom Cruise of course, who now sticks around so long he's actually starting to weird out even his most devoted fans.

After appearing in their own cartoon series, the Smurfs turned to drag racing.

Dyke Jumping

Despite its seemingly provocative name, Dyke Jumping does not involve leaping over successively taller and wider lesbians. It's a sport that's been practised for as long as dykes, poles and idiots have been around.

Country of Origin: Netherlands

Possibility of death or serious injury: Death is rare, but broken limbs, dislocations and lost clogs are frequent.

Embarrassing clothing: Not strictly necessary, but as with the London Marathon there's always a few dressed like complete tools.

Greatest hazard: Splinters and severe gastric disorders.

Watch out for: The Flying Dutchman.

Prize/Rewards: Competition to find immortality on the Dyke Jumping Roll of Honour is not so fierce as you might think. Most people just do it because they're prats.

People most likely to enjoy it: People who'd like to make some friends. Alright just one would do.

Expect to hear: "Who told you it was OK to put your finger there?"

History

Dyke jumping owes its roots to the skills perfected by farmers back in the days when their animals didn't live out their entire tragic existence locked in industrial-size warehouses. Dutch and Belgian farmers would graze their herds in fields delineated by dykes, not fences. When checking on their animals they took a handy pole to avoid getting their clogs and trousers wet. The sport is known across Europe as Fierrljeppen, or Far Leaping – a misleading name on two counts since leaping doesn't traditionally involve the use of a great pole, and few of the competitors make it very far. Still, it

does provide harmless fun for the spectators, the vast majority of whom aren't there to watch feats of remarkable athleticism and are much more interested in the kind of slapstick comedy made popular by Buster Keaton. It draws its competitors from an endless pool of *You've Been Framed* wannabes who are all too happy to be centre of attention for a few brief seconds. These witless cretins are prepared to endure the seemingly minor but frequently very painful injuries along with the trips to the hospital for stomach pumping that are the occupational hazards of this daft pastime.

You'll Need...

A dyke, ditch, canal, trench, river or similar. A large pole, between 3m and 5m in length, with a flat base to prevent it from sinking into the muddy base of whatever it is you're attempting to jump. Though since the whole *raison d'etre* of this sport seems to be the humiliation of its participants it's a little strange that they draw the line there. Given this you'll also need a healthy sense of humour and an injection for Weil's disease (carried by water rats).

Advanced

Despite it being far less entertaining, the Dutch inventors of the sport maintain that dyke jumping is a serious business and even have records for the longest ever jumps, the current senior length standing at over 20m. Which just goes to show the kind of crazy stuff that goes on in societies that legalise cannabis.

Why You Shouldn't Bother

Dyke jumping has a great deal to offer. The spectator. Take a video camera with you.

Endurance Motorsport

Le Mans, Gumball and the others are designed to test three things – the durability of machinery and equipment, the stamina of crew and driver and, above all, the endurance of the viewing audience.

Country of Origin: USA

Possibility of death or serious injury: It's a high-speed motorsport for the sleep-deprived. Go figure.

Embarrassing clothing: The kind of tight leather all-in-one that Freddie Mercury used to favour.

Greatest hazard: Listening to "The Bedtime Soft Jazz Hour" on the car stereo.

Watch out for: Out of control cars spinning by with the driver curled up on the back seat.

People most likely to enjoy it: Anyone with excellent bladder control who enjoys going round and round in a Ford Mondeo for hours on end.

Expect to hear: "The last eight hours of the race are the ones that really drag"

Someone's pimped this ride.

History

Boys and their toys. No sooner had the workings of the internal combustion engine been finessed to the point that it no longer required a guttersnipe to run ahead waving a red flag than someone suggested it might be fun to race a couple of them. Actually they would have said "*jolie*" because *Grand Prix* racing started in France. Hence the name. And in less time than it takes to punch a hole in the ozone layer someone else had the brainwave that what would make such a race really fun would be if the entrants were to stay up all night doing it. And so the first in a proposed schedule of 24-hour races took place at the newly opened Brooklands racetrack in 1907. Understandable complaints from the residents sadly led to it being the last in the schedule, with the next race competed over two blocks of 12 hours, which kind of missed the point of the whole 24-hour endurance thing. Still, these early teething troubles with the format couldn't ultimately keep it down, and since then endurance motorsport has now filled out an impressive calendar of events, dominated by the Triple Crown: 24 Hours of Daytona, 12 Hours of Sebring and 24 Hours of Le Mans, making a colossal total of 60 hours of high speed racing; that no one watches.

You'll Need...

A car. In contrast to F1, the objective in choosing a vehicle is not pure speed but a combination of pace, reliability and fuel efficiency. In fact, fans claim that one of the sport's key appeals is the trickle down effect that happens between the vehicles used in these inexplicably prestigious events and the kind of model you can be overcharged for at your local dealership.

How You Do It

One of the techniques of endurance motorsport that has clearly trickled down to the everyday driver is the Le Mans start. Head out to Melbourne's commuter belt just before 6am on a weekday morning and you'll see legions of harassed drivers sprinting to their cars whilst simultaneously necking cups of espresso, extinguishing cigarettes and hastily doing their trousers up. Le Mans hosts between 60,000 and 80,000 British fans every year, who crowd out the cross-Channel ferries from the week before till the week after the event. Bemused motorists can arrive at Calais or Ouistreham on the Wednesday evening (after the race ended on Sunday) and find Ford Transit minibuses with all the passengers standing on the roof drinking beer and playing air guitar. Two words, "Le Mans", explains it all. Of the 80,000 visitors, only seven watch the race, while 79,993 watch the start and the finish and then try to avoid watching it for the 23 hours in between. There's a host of entertainments set up for the fans including a fairground, bars and restaurants. On returning from the Le Mans weekend (week/fortnight) it's traditional not to remember who won the race: "...but I think he was driving the Audi."

Advanced

The Le Mans start inevitably led to crashes, so the preferred method for starting now is the rolling, or Indianapolis start. This looks a lot like normal motorway driving, with the pace car playing the role of a police car that's just come into view. Cars maintain a healthy distance from each other and regulate their speed to that set by the pace car. And, as in real life, once the pace car disappears it's business as usual and drivers can return to the mayhem, crashes and general carnage that the race's audience has tuned in for.

Why You Shouldn't Bother

A really close finish is when one of the cars finishes within ten minutes of another. Exciting, eh? And the anti-climaxes can be massive. Imagine preparing for weeks for the race and then losing the car on the second lap. If your idea of fun really *is* spending 24 hours behind the wheel of your car maybe you should try getting round the M25 on a bank holiday weekend.

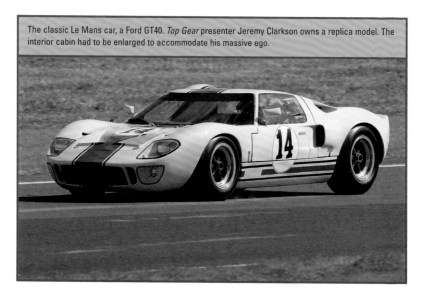

The classic Le Mans car, a Ford GT40. *Top Gear* presenter Jeremy Clarkson owns a replica model. The interior cabin had to be enlarged to accommodate his massive ego.

Eton Wall Game

The most important game of the school year is played on St. Andrew's Day, by teams determined along traditional demarcations – scholars versus non-scholars, stupid and rich versus intelligent and poor.

Country of Origin: England

Possibility of death or serious injury: Any injuries up to actual death are considered character-building and actively encouraged.

Embarrassing clothing: Not when you see the kind of clobber they have to wear through the streets of Eton.

Greatest hazard: Debagging with extreme prejudice.

Watch out for: Sir in the showers afterwards.

Prize/Rewards: Giving the other boys a "damn good licking".

People most likely to enjoy it: The kind of sadomasochistic future parliamentarians who will be quite happy to take the party whip.

Expect to hear: "Has anybody seen an ear? I've lorst my ear."

One cannot get one's fag to participate for one. One has to make contact oneself with the lower orders.

History

Founded in 1440 as a charity to provide education to poor boys, Eton college is now essentially a hatchling area for mercenary captains of industry, witless royals and bumbling politicians. And their kids. At £9,000 a term it doesn't come cheap. In keeping with its quintessentially English nature, Eton is responsible for at least three sports the rest of the world has no understanding of. The Field Game and Fives are knocked into a top hat by the Eton Wall Game, a sport which is brutal, muddy and pointless, but where the participants swear with very nice accents.

You'll Need...

To be at Eton. The essential exclusivity of the sport starts with the fact that there's only one place on the planet you can actually play it, a strip of ground next to the curved brick wall on College Field.

How You Do It

The object of the game is to move the ball towards your opponent's end of the pitch. In doing this, the scholars have the advantage of being on home turf – however, this benefits them only theoretically since in practice the non-scholars are allowed to use it whenever they wish.

Why You Shouldn't Bother

After an hour or so of this mayhem the game is over. No one will have scored. No one ever does. But everyone will feel good about the fact that they have taken part in a centuries' old tradition. There will be cheering and caps will be tossed in the air. And then the boys will return to their dorms and cry into their pillows, vowing that they will never send their kids away to school.

Extreme Ironing

Demanding cardiovascular fitness, stamina and strength as well as an eye for a nicely executed crease; extreme ironing is the perfect all-round sport for those who like to push household chores to their physical limits.

Country of Origin: Great Britain

Possibility of death or serious injury: All extreme sports carry a high level of risk. Here, the danger is slightly lower if you use a setting for delicates.

Embarrassing clothing: Not at all. In fact everything will be beautifully neat and crisply pressed.

Greatest hazard: Running out of hangers during the final ascent.

People most likely to enjoy it: Practical jokers.

Potential expansion: A handful of pioneering women are currently working around the clock to perfect the Spin Cycle Rodeo event.

Expect to hear: "Getting to the top of the Eiger wasn't half as tough as finding an extension lead with a 4,000-metre cord."

History

Recent urban legend has it that extreme ironing was invented by a put-upon Leicester factory worker by the name of Phil Shaw. Coming home from a hard day at work, and depressed not only by the city of Leicester itself, but by the fact that he had a pile of domestic chores awaiting him, he decided to combine one of his most thankless menial tasks with one of his favourite sporting pastimes – rock climbing. One promotional world tour, a book deal, a TV show and accompanying DVD later and extreme ironing had established itself at the vanguard of a sport that has been with us for centuries, but which is becoming more and more sophisticated, and growing rapidly in popularity. Namely, winding up those elements of the media whose desire to find "news bulletin quirky stories" has led them to occupy a position of such blinkeredness they can't actually tell when they're being wound up.

You'll Need…

An iron and ironing board. Three major schools of thought have emerged on what constitutes the ideal equipment. The first is that it's worth investing in high performance equipment that combines lightness with durability, which can be relied upon in even the most adverse of conditions and which carries features such as a self-cleaning soleplate, drop resistance and a high level of continuous steam output to ensure that the garments are pressed to the highest possible standards. The second school asserts that the hostile environments you're likely to find yourself in will render your kit unusable upon completion of your attempt, regardless of its quality, and therefore it makes sense to only invest in materials good enough to get the job done. The third school insists that the standard of the iron and board is irrelevant since extreme ironing doesn't actually exist. What all schools do agree on is that the iron used must be battery powered, since the option of using a mains socket for your ironing session will automatically render your attempt anything but extreme. Indeed, the scion of extreme ironing known as underwater ironing would be overly hazardous if it involved passing a live 240 volt electricity supply into the local swimming pool.

How You Do It

What is certainly refreshing about extreme ironing is that its governing body – the Extreme Ironing Bureau – have proved highly accommodating in allowing the membership of the community to shape the future direction of the sport. In marked contrast to many of the world's sporting authorities, the EIB has been neither dogged by scandals, nor scandalised by dogging. It has been suggested that one of the reasons the sport is so good-natured at every level, from ruling body to casual follower, is that its audience exists only in cyberspace – extreme ironing events are not attended by spectators, but viewed remotely, usually via the internet. Whether this is the case or not, it may explain why British Premiership clubs are embarking on their current strategy of pricing fans out of the stadiums, building fan bases thousands of miles from the teams' locations and relocating games on the other side of the planet.

Advanced

The experienced ironers are all quick to point out that they travel with support teams who provide back-up and maintain constant contact in the event of anything going wrong. However, novices should never, ever answer a cell phone once they've started their attempt.

Why You Shouldn't Bother

The questions surrounding the actual existence of extreme ironing as a sport are in many ways redundant. Whether we take Plato's view that the presence of structures and symbols that we do not or cannot comprehend can be explained by locating them in what Plato labels higher or abstract forms, or we take the more contemporary phenomenal realist view that anything incorporated into the fabric of human existence as we experience it is therefore by definition real, we're talking about ironing. Which is never, ever enjoyable. That's why we have dry cleaners.

Unlucky for some.

Fencing

It takes a lot of effort to make sword-fighting boring, but with Herculean effort fencers and the sport's regulatory body have managed to reduce an exciting spectacle to the point where it looks like two iPod ear plugs waving pins at each other.

Country of Origin: France
Possibility of death or serious injury: Chance would be a fine thing. Statistically, fencing is now safer than settling down in a comfy chair to read the paper.
Embarrassing clothing: Yes, a kind of ballet outfit in white, though once you tie the kitchen sieve to your face no one will recognize you.
Prize/Rewards: Not so much. The days of impressive facial scars and killing people so you can get off with their wife (or killing people because you got off with their wife) are long gone.
People most likely to enjoy it: Those who secretly believe that they were one of the three musketeers in a previous life.
Potential expansion: Considerable potential among teenage hoodies who like doing some damage with a blade.
Expect to hear: "En Garde… Pret?…Allez!…Owwwww!"

History

It is one of only four sports that featured in the first modern Olympic Games of 1896 and is still around today. Fencing is with us thanks to the noble, honourable and frankly much-missed tradition of upper-class idiots killing each other in duels. The modern version of the sport is conducted by athletes from all over the world, but its jargon and technical names all have to be delivered in that most cutting of languages, *Francais*. Preferably with a the kind of Gallic sneer visitors to Paris will have encountered a dozen times before they've even made it out of the Eurostar terminal.

You'll Need…

A fencing foil. Crucially, this is not defined as being a sword and was developed in France during the eighteenth century as a light training weapon designed purely for precision rather than the hack and slash conventionally administered by the working man at arms. Whether you choose to use a light foil, a more sturdy *épée* or the cutting style design of a sabre, you'll need a button on the end to stop you puncturing anyone's lung. Although if you're not careful and someone's forgotten their safety mask you could probably still have someone's eye out, button or no button. You'll also need tight trousers, a tight tunic and fencing shoes, which have an excellent grip but tend to be more lightweight than conventional trainers. You should ensure that all of these items are pristine and white. Wear black clothing and you'll be taken for a fencing master or coach. Alternatively, once you've got your mask on people will probably just assume you're on your way to a fancy dress party dressed as a microphone.

Don't forget to come armed with insults, too. To make the contest very French try thinking up insults about your opponent's cuisine.

How You Do It

Lower body strength is the key to success in modern fencing. Lunging, thrusting and similarly dirty sounding words are the things you'll need to master if you're going to get anywhere, although slackers could just plump for the option favoured by Olympic contestant Colonel Boris Onischenko who just rigged his foil up to record hits he never made at the 1976 Olympics, thus securing his own special place in the ranks of the history of cheating at the Games. Though anyone who's witnessed the tedium of an expert bout might think that in messing with the wiring he was onto something, and that connecting both blades to a mains current might actually pep things up a bit in terms of entertainment value.

Advanced

Fencing was once inextricably linked to the honour of the two combatants. The sharp decline in duelling in the early part of the twentieth century has left us with a highly technical and bone dry sport bereft of any links to the things that made duelling such a compelling spectacle. The sport's governing body does seem to have recognised that if fencing is to survive it needs to take the sport back to a time when it was closer to its roots.

Why You Shouldn't Bother

Despite (or maybe because) Iron Maiden's Bruce Dickinson is a keen fencer, the sport is dying on its arse. What the fencing federation needs to inject is a bit more showbiz. They can make exciting films about musketeers, they *can't* do the same for 3,000-metre hurdlers, so it's got a natural advantage. In future, contests should be held on castle battlements or in oak-panelled banqueting halls with specially installed chandeliers to swing from. Taking inspiration from Cyrano de Bergerac, contestants will also be required to trade verbal insults in French with marks awarded for use of language, smugness of tone and quivering of eyebrow on delivery. And both swordsmen have to wear big flouncy shirts and false noses.

The thrill of fencing can last up to several seconds.

Finger Jousting

Finger Jousting is a bizarre hybrid of fencing, wrestling and the kind of snidey sibling combat that those of us not lucky enough to be born an only child will be all too familiar with.

Country of Origin: USA

Possibility of death or serious injury: Some caution recommended. Overly aggressive finger jousting can lead to injuries that may affect your ability to pick your nose.

Watch out for: Double-jointed opponents.

Prize/Rewards: Not in the same league as Formula One, but a similar buzz can be attained by standing on a chair and spraying your opponent with a heavily shaken can of Coke.

People most likely to enjoy it: Very, very, very bored people who can't get out. Students.

Potential expansion: Plans are underway to form a Championship Pro-Goosing competition and a World Chinese Burn League.

Expect to hear: "Owwww! Cut your nails, dude!"

History

The fraternity system of American college campuses is as old as the country itself. Membership of a frat is restricted according to athletic prowess, attractiveness to the opposite sex, or familial wealth, connections and power. So no mystery as to which category a certain George Jr used to make it into the notoriously influential Skull and Bones fraternity, an institution at Yale since 1832. Those that don't make it into one of these cliquey little clubs build their lives around non-stop partying and find alternative, counter

cultural ways to express themselves and build social networks. Fantasy role playing game circles, religious groups, Sandra Bullock appreciation societies. But a very special few will find that nothing on earth will meet their own very special needs, and be compelled to invent a brand new sport…

You'll Need…

Your right hand with a fully functioning set of four fingers and one thumb. This makes the sport appealing to teenage boys of every background since it's something that most teenage boys are not only in possession of, it's also the one part of their developing frames that gets frequent doses of regular exercise and is therefore unusually highly developed.

How You Do It

Right hands must be locked in a slight variation on the arm wrestling style – so it's not a sport for southpaws.

Advanced

The sport's governing body – the WFJF – very helpfully supplies not merely the rules of the sport on its informative and amusing public website, but also its history, and suggestions for the essential elements that make a good match. These include the excellent idea that all jousts be conducted with a deal/prize to be awarded to the victor at the conclusion of the bout – making finger jousting a far closer relative to good old-fashioned duelling. It doesn't list proposals but you might consider jousting for the right to rename your defeated opponent for the rest of the day, or to force him/her/it to eat a whole jar of mustard. Or something equally mature.

Footbag Net

Keeping an old bag in the air for as long as possible may look pointless to anyone who isn't Madonna's travel agent, but smoke enough dope and pretty much anything can seem like fun.

Country of Origin: Thailand

Possibility of death or serious injury: The potential of a small bag of dried beans as an offensive weapon may seem slight, but in the hands of an enraged hippy the hacky sack can cause severe discomfort, especially when the contents are used to make a vegetarian chilli.

Embarrassing clothing: Baggy tie-dyed pants and T-shirts often printed with yin-yang symbols or magic mushrooms.

Greatest hazard: A small dispute can quickly turn into a bad vibe. Serious karmic bummer, man.

Prize/Rewards: Traditionally the winners get to "spark up" a celebratory bong. This can last for weeks or minutes, depending on what your perception of the universe is.

People most likely to enjoy it: Non bread-heads. Beach bums who can't afford jet skis or swing ball.

Expect to hear: "Way to go, Mountain Rainforest Dew, nice shot!"

"Woah, dude! I'm a happy hacky sack. Try and keep me in the air."

History

Whilst the precise origins of kicking around a little "hacky sack" beanbag are unknown, the 1970s relaunch captured the imaginations of a generation of hippies, drop-outs, mime artists and other sporting failures. They saw the co-operative nature and non-judgemental spirit of hackin' the sack – keeping it in the air around a circle – as a metaphor for the way they wished to live their lives. A successful circuit was completed when the sack makes it round the group, being touched by every player at least once. All of which was very 1970s. Then, with all the chutzpah you'd expect from the guy in marketing that nobody likes, it was suggested, "Wouldn't it be a bit more fun if there was a net too?" And that, rather than trying as one collective group to keep the footbag aloft, it might give things a bit more of a fun edge if the group was split into two teams with each team attempting to force the other to lose control of the sack and drop it. And so the sport of footbag net was born, and the original spirit of the game pissed all over.

How You Do It

Footbag is essentially a pointless addition to the volleyball/badminton oeuvre, where teams have a maximum of three touches to return the hack. Teams compete to be the first to 15 points, or by two clear points beyond that. Though frankly we are talking about people who are into hacky sack. If it gets to that stage with a group of people so obviously raised in the competitive-sports-free environment most hippies favour, one of three things will happen: most likely the group will get out a guitar, make a bonfire from the net, and go back to playing hacky sack the good old co-operative way.

Formula One

"A modern Formula One car has almost as much in common with a jet fighter as it does with an ordinary road car", it says here on this F1 promotional material. That means you're going to need cash, and a lot of it.

Country of Origin: Conglomerate of European Business Interests

Possibility of death or serious injury: Yes, to which you can add the possibility of ending up looking like a human/tortoise hybrid (see N. Lauda).

Embarrassing clothing: You'll look like a billboard, but will be so rich and sexually satisfied that you won't care.

Greatest hazard: Piles. To get to F1 you'll have to spend your time in suspension-less go-karts from the age of eight, move on to suspension-less F3 cars, GP2 cars and virtually rigid F1 cars where the only give is in the tyres. That's a lot of punishment.

Prize/Rewards: Money, fame, hot girls and all the champagne you can waste. A $50 million salary allows drivers to scratch a living.

People most likely to enjoy it: Short people, as they're the only ones who can fit in the cars. Tall drivers such as Robert Kubica and Mark Webber are at a distinct disadvantage because they have to go on the Japanese POW camp diet to compete.

Expect to hear: "And on Lap 76 it's still the same order as the opening lap."

History

Formula One is the highest class of open wheeled motor racing in the world. You'll know it's high class because it has a race in Monaco and is presided over by a very small man with a beautiful trophy wife. The president of the sport's governing body had a secret penchant for being whipped by dominatrices in dungeons, that is until he was exposed in the *News of the World*. It's the most political sport in the world and there are two separate World Championships. There's the official one where the drivers race each other for the world title. Then there's the one where the sport's governing body, the FIA, races to adapt the rules to make sure that Ferrari win and that McLaren don't. Imagine if the governing body of football, FIFA, had a place on the committee reserved for Manchester United. F1 is like that.

You'll Need...

A Ferrari. Anything else is just making up the numbers. Even the multi-billion dollar investment from Japanese car giants Toyota and Honda has only brought them a handful of wins and podiums, plus a crushing end to the slogan "The car in front is a Toyota". Normally, the smoking car parked at the end of the pitlane is a Toyota. Whereas Honda's adoption of the slogan "Earth Dreams" has seen them slump so badly people assume they're testing out new technology for motobility vehicles.

How You Do It

F1 races are a bit like war. Nothing happens for ages, they all follow each other round, and then loads of things happen, it ends and then everybody argues about the result. At some races, nothing happens at all. You can guarantee that there will be no overtaking at Imola, Barcelona, Valencia, Magny Cours and Monza. The rules of Formula One are in a near constant state of flux as the authorities seek to balance the impact of new technologies with

Lewis Hamilton has rocked the F1 establishment, showing genuine signs of trying to overtake people.

the demands of the huge viewing audience. The most recent rule changes have largely sought to promote more overtaking. What is clear is that however the rules change, the very best drivers excel across a wide range of skill sets. Michael Schumacher – aka The Red Baron, Schumi, Schu, Celine Dion – has frequently been cited as the greatest driver the sport has ever seen, and he perhaps embodies the combination of supreme athleticism, tactical nous and precision driving skills required to compete at the very highest level in this sport. Understanding that colliding with your opponents in the last race of the season when you're leading the championship on points has also been a feature of his career … as well as swerving into people, brake testing them in corners, deliberately blocking the track in qualifying, trying to get races stopped and

making his team-mate move over to give him race wins. His father says he was never the same after he watched a Dick Dastardly cartoon as a child. Today, the Lewis Hamilton, Felipe Massa and Sebastian Vettel generation has taken over and get along with each other a lot better. The days of Nigel Mansell gently lifting Ayrton Senna up by the throat in the pits are long gone. Sadly.

Why You Shouldn't Bother

When you can simulate the exact experience of a Grand Prix using the X-Box or PlayStation 3 there's really not much point. And do you really want all that bother of a yacht in Monaco, beautiful women throwing themselves at you, international brand managers fighting for your signature and the best things that money can buy…?

Fox Hunting

Fox hunting is illegal in the U.K. now. The banning has actually proved immensely popular, particularly in rural parts where the folk like nothing better than getting advice on how to run their affairs by a collection of frappacino-drinking urbanites who wouldn't know one end of a badger from the other.

Country of Origin: England

Possibility of death or serious injury: Apoplectic rage at killjoy townies has caused numerous strokes.

Embarrassing clothing: If you have a shapely backside, then everyone will be too busy staring at it in tight jodhpurs to notice that the rest of you looks a pillock.

Watch out for: Police, hunt saboteurs and the National Midgets' Rambling Society.

Prize/Rewards: The thrill of the chase, the joy of the kill and the ecstasy of having your face rubbed with a mangy fox tail covered in blood.

People most likely to enjoy it: Country la-di-das for whom croquet has ceased to fulfill the desire for cruelty.

Potential expansion: With fox populations on the rise in metropolitan areas urban fox hunting has been suggested as a culling measure. And New-Labour-MP-hunting has been suggested as "damn good fun".

Expect to hear: "Tally Ho!"

History

For as long as there's been a food chain, the human race has sat near the top of it – not getting eaten by things that could get above it in the rankings, and eating everything below. Obviously there have been exceptions to this throughout history. Shark fin soup is still highly prized in the Far East, and we stopped eating tigers once they agreed to start sharing their breakfast cereal with us. But as man has got fussier in his tastes there has evolved a new category of animal – ones which we'd rather not eat, but which we don't want to take over the place. Some of these have proved useful to man in other ways. Horses can be ridden, set to work in the fields, or raced. Dogs can guard our dwellings, sniff out narcotic substances and take blind people for walks. And cats can…well, do just whatever it is that cats do to earn their keep: lie around and occasionally pester you for affection until you're actually willing to stroke them, at which point they'll ignore the new recipe food you put out to go and have group orgies on the rooftop that keep you up all night. Anyway, foxes have proved about as useful to man as, well, cats come to think of it. But while the domestic moggy's worst crime is thinking you'll appreciate a freshly slaughtered starling artfully laid out on the kitchen tiles, foxes like nothing better than making off with the chickens and pheasants that we've earmarked for ourselves. And so, fox hunting was born – the epic confrontation between the lone, wily fox and the resolute and steadfast huntsman. And his 50 or so mates. And their horses. And a few dogs, well, a pack really. And some guns. Plus a horn that makes a noise like an old water bottle expiring.

You'll Need…

Fox hunting is an elaborate affair. The act of getting rid of pests may traditionally be a grimy one, but fox hunting is anything but. You'll need a bunch of fancy clothes, including a nice scarlet jacket, English dress boots and ribbons

Hunting real foxes is banned in the U.K. now, so instead a bloke dresses up in a smelly fox costume. To give an added layer of needle he phones the huntsmen up and taunts them.

which are worn up or down depending on whether you are professional or amateur in status. You'll probably want to pack a change of clothes for when your hunting attire gets covered in the tin of red paint the hunt protesters brought along with your name on it.

How You Do It

Bizarrely, the new improved fox-friendly system introduced as a result of the hunting act of 2004, where hunts follow an artificially laid trail, has actually led to an increase in attendances. And no foxes die, oh no.

Advanced

Certain elements of a traditional hunt – such as the "blooding" of new huntsmen – have had to be abandoned due to the fact that since the act

was passed, no hunt has been responsible for the death of a single fox. However, there has been a remarkable increase in roadkill, a large percentage of which has been found in the middle of muddy fields, dense forest and other locations notable for their lack of road traffic.

Why You Shouldn't Bother

If you're really into slaughtering defenceless creatures there's still a million ways of doing it legally that don't require you to work in an abattoir. And while the government succeeded in introducing legislation that's not only made the sport more popular but also proved virtually impossible for the police to enforce, chances are your fun is still likely to be spoilt by a pack of saboteurs with worse personal hygiene than the foxes they're trying to protect.

The traditional view of fox hunters was that they were "the unspeakable chasing the uneatable". These days it's the unspeakable chasing the uncatchable.

Freediving

All forms of diving are inherently dangerous, and their practitioners therefore essentially stupid. However, the sport of freediving has succeeded in making all other forms of diving look positively mundane by comparison.

Country of Origin: USA

Possibility of death or serious injury: Yes, expect your life insurance premiums to outstrip any possible earnings.

Embarrassing clothing: No, many people love the idea of being mistaken for a seal or an anorexic dolphin.

Greatest hazard: A sudden flash of realization, at 200m, that what you're doing is actually really stupid and dangerous. And sharks of course.

Watch out for: Interesting new species of tubeworms.

Prize/Rewards: Tanya Streeter, the ever-so-slightly-gorgeous holder of many women's freediving records is so famous in her native Turks and Caicos Islands that she's been put on the stamps – making her the only woman apart from the Virgin Mary and the royal family to appear on them. She'd probably prefer the cash, though.

People most likely to enjoy it: Those who gave up their fins for legs when they fell in love with a human.

Expect to hear: Whales, 700 miles away. Noisy bastards.

History

Freediving evolved to offer its exponents what is often somewhat coyly described as "the chance to dive without the assistance or encumbrance of breathing apparatus". Which to any sane person would sound about as appealing as skydiving without the assistance or encumbrance of a parachute.

You'll Need...

Your lungs, obviously. Of course, we've all had a bit of fun seeing who can hold their breath for longest in the shallow end, but freediving takes the whole hold-your-nose-and-stick-your-head-underwater competition to its most insane extremes, employing as it does teams of technicians to construct guide lines to drag divers down to the bottom of the ocean on weighted sleds. Many divers employ a monofin to help them back to the surface on the return

Freediving to some is like a near-religious experience. Probably because it's like a near-death experience.

So-called freediving actually has many hidden costs...such as an expedition team.

leg of their misguided trip. This adds further weight to the theory that many of freediving's most vocal advocates are deluded crackpots who are simply biding time until medical technology has advanced far enough for them to be species-reassigned as dolphins.

How You Do It

The Mammalian Diving Reflex is key to understanding how freedivers are able to endure water pressure and oxygen deprivation far beyond typical endurance levels. By accustoming their muscles to work under anaerobic conditions and increasing their tolerance of CO_2, and by hyperventilating for brief periods prior to a dive, freedivers are able to coax their bodies into a state of bradycardia. Their heartbeats drop as low as 50bpm, and as they relax into states nearing physical suspension, their blood vessels shrink and shift away from their limbs. Brain activity drops, and in medical terms they are in a state of torpor that means they are barely alive. Non freedivers can experience this remarkable phenomenon simply by settling in for the night in front of the *Scary Movie* trilogy. However, as with freediving, it is important that you don't do it alone. Make sure you have a "buddy" standing by to pull you out – i.e. hit the disc eject button – should your brain activity start to flatline completely.

Why You Shouldn't Bother

The depth record currently stands at a staggering 244m. Think you can top that? No, exactly. There are some records that are made to be broken (mostly by Cliff) but this isn't one of them. However, should you wish to join the glitterati of the breath-holding world – Tanya Streeter can do it for over six minutes – this is a sport you can practise at home in the bath. It's probably a lot better to figure out you can't make it past the two-minute mark lying stationary in a nice warm tub than after you've been dragged halfway to the ocean floor. In which case you can go back to one of the other fun solo activities you can do in the bath. Like playing with rubber ducks. Or farting.

Golf

Golf isn't just for swingers, it's also for flabby-arsed, DIY-shirkers who think that tartan jumpers and beige slacks are acceptable modes of dress.

Country of Origin: Scotland

Possibility of death or serious injury: Not until the green staff stop pussying around. The Royal and Ancient make it quite clear that anti-personnel mines are allowed in out-of-bounds areas and non-implementation is just encouraging the kind of slack play that's dragging the game down.

Embarrassing clothing: The very worst. Most embarrassing sports clothing is there for a function, but golf gear masquerades as being everyday leisurewear and "normal"... just as Harold Shipman was a normal GP.

Greatest hazard: Opinions differ. Some say sand, others say water. Most 24+ handicaps say any kind of tree on a golf course is a hazard.

Watch out for: The birdie.

Prize/Rewards: The avoidance of visiting relations at weekends and fiddly little DIY jobs.

People most likely to enjoy it: The fashionably challenged. Golf can be a test of how poor your choice of clothes is. If you look at golf clothes and think, "Hmm, I could wear those Farah slacks outside the golf course," then you know you're beyond redemption.

Potential expansion: Not in Queensland until they get some more water. It's difficult to see how golf could get any bigger unless Jack Nicklaus landscapes the whole of Spain and Florida.

Expect to hear: "FORE!"

Many golfers prefer to play at twilight so they can't be spotted in their golf clothes.

History

A love of deep-frying food and a long-harboured hatred for the English aside, China and Scotland share little in the way of cultural heritage. However, both of these remarkable nations can lay claim to the game that we know as golf, some time in the eleventh century. But while the Chinese didn't manage to hang onto their scorecard – thus invalidating their claim – the Scots are able to produce records of a game played in 1456. That coupled with the fact that per head of population there is a golf course for every household in Scotland, while China has a single putting green available to its 1.2 billion population (located in the Zhongnanhai and for the sole use of senior party officials), is enough for any neutral to recognise that the modern game is one that's clearly of Scottish design. Scotland can also lay claim to the game's oldest course at Musselburgh, although it's fair to say that in its early days the modern game was somewhat different from the game we know and are forced to tolerate today. The world famous St Andrews course may seem an idyllic and well-tended spot now, but in the sixteenth century a round of 22 holes was a somewhat wilder affair. Players would set off into the wilderness in search of the holes armed with just a putter and a Mashie-Niblick and would often not return for days.

You'll Need…

The game has certainly come a long way since its early days, and golf can now lay claim to being the most over-equipped sport in the modern world. You'll need a bag full of stuff little of which you'll know what to do with and most of which you won't use. You'll also need to wear the kind of clothes that would have got you beaten up had your parents ever made you wear them to school. Perhaps it's no great surprise to learn that half of the planet's 32,000 golf courses are to be found in the USA, which is just what you'd expect of a sport so clearly built around conspicuous consumption. Modern innovations such as the golf cart and motorised bag means that in the words of Mark Twain there isn't even a good walk to ruin any more.

How You Do It

Successful golf is all about striking a balance between power and precision, which shouldn't be too much of a dilemma for the novice player who is unlikely to have either. Start with the biggest club you can find in your bag and try not to think too hard about the players waiting behind you and mentally willing you to make an idiot of yourself by shanking your ball five yards off the tee.

Advanced

Golf has a handicap system which in theory should allow players of different abilities to compete at similar levels. In practice it's the best way to cheat yourself into a result. Men's handicaps start at 1 and go up to 24; women's go up to 36, highlighting an area where women are in no rush to make themselves equal. Women might want equal opportunities but they're quite happy to tee off on special ladies' tees which are placed so close to the hole they might as well be playing on a pitch-and-putt course. "Ladies" of course is a euphemism for the kind of blue-rinsed, Lexus-driving old biddy you might find in a Gary Larson cartoon.

Why You Shouldn't Bother

Golf is not going to make you fit. It's not going to make you happy. It's not going to make you new friends – if you're good they're jealous, if you're bad you're embarrassing. And it's not going to impress women unless you can introduce them to Tiger Woods.

American vehicle researchers are trying to devise a buggy where golfers can play a whole round without having to stand up.

Gymnastics

There are as many kinds of gymnastic disciplines as there are muscles, joints and bones in your body for you to do irreparable damage to.

Country of Origin: Greece

Possibility of death or serious injury: Death is rare but it is not unknown for limbs stretched beyond normal limits to suddenly snap off.

Embarrassing clothing: Doing the splits upside down in an outfit tighter than your own skin has a certain "nothing left to the imagination" factor.

Watch out for: Puberty.

Prize/Rewards: One or two, like Olga Corbett, become legends, the rest will flick-flack their way into obscurity as emotional and physical wrecks.

People most likely to enjoy it: Rubber people and circus freaks.

Expect to hear: "If it doesn't hurt, you can't be doing it right."

History

By AD 393 the Olympic Games had already been running for a thousand years and were riven with corruption. Roman Emperor Theodosius is considered by many classical scholars to have been right in his decision to abolish them. Leaving aside the small matter of crucifying the son of god and then chucking his followers to the lions for a few hundred years after that, the Romans certainly managed to get a few things right. We could probably do with someone fulfilling the emperor's role for us today. With the end of the games, the training of athletes in the gymnasia gave way to the rise of exercises based around military training. Fifteen hundred years later it took a couple of Germans who'd spent a lot of time looking at the physical development of young boys – to an extent that would probably lead to

a raid by social services these days – to come up with the apparatus we know and despise today. With the introduction of parallel bars, vaulting horses and horizontal bars, men's gymnastics were included in the first modern Olympic Games in 1896. It was another 30 years before women's gymnastics got in on the act, due largely to the misguided standards in morality that were all too prevalent at the time. When ladies were finally included, there were still calls from an outraged and highly vocal sector of the populace who disapproved of the scandalous attire female gymnasts wore to compete in. These highly provocative garments allowed men to see the shape of their ankles and catch the odd erotic glimpse of calf.

You'll Need...

For acrobatic gymnastics, such as floor work, you'll need a piece of music, although restrictions do exist on choice – performers may not be accompanied by music with lyrics, music that has over 90 beats per minute, music that is copyrighted to the Disney organisation, arrangements involving a banjo or anything by James Blunt, no matter how incidental. Performers are recommended to avoid music that has strong visual connotations, such as the Benny Hill kazoo chase music.

In the days of the old Soviet Bloc, ruthless East German gym trainers would use the tickling stick at this point.

How You Do It

Gymnastics is a collective term for a wide range of disciplines, each of which requires different abilities. Vault requires running at speed then somersaulting forwards. Beam requires balancing on a narrow beam and somersaulting backwards or forwards. Floor requires running at speed and somersaulting forwards, then twisting your hand in an artistic way to show that even though you've got the thighs of a rugby prop forward you can do art. Asymmetric bars involve somersaulting between two bars of differing height, which look about as sturdy as something your dad put up on that camping weekend from hell when the tent blew away.

Advanced

Special mention should go to Team Gym, a Scandinavian invention where teams of six to 12 gymnasts perform sequences on the floor, trampette and vaulting horses. From a spectator's point of view it can be great fun to watch as all it takes is a mistake by one member of the team to make the whole edifice of team harmony come crashing down in lemming-like catastrophe. This also supplies yet another reason not to get involved.

Landing a backward somersault on the beam is only slightly easier than landing a space shuttle.

Why You Shouldn't Bother

Gymnastics is truly a sport than can claim to do more harm than good. The good news is that unless you're a six-year-old with an unhealthily high pain threshold and a 45-hour gap in your weekly diary, no serious trainer will be interested in taking you on anyway.

In China, gymnasts are trained from the age of four to 14, when they automatically become 16 to make them eligible for international competitions.

Handball

Anyone, or anything, that insists on telling you how popular they are is clearly flawed at a very deep level. That is of course the case with this sport, or anyone who plays it.

Country of Origin: No one has owned up yet so it might as well be Germany.

Possibility of death or serious injury: A few breaks and bruises. So nothing interesting there.

Embarrassing clothing: A remarkably restrained shorts and T-shirt combo that should look OK on anyone except the morbidly obese.

Watch out for: Massive worldwide indifference.

Prize/Rewards: Various international tournaments offer highly prized medals and trophies, and pretty much bugger all else.

People most likely to enjoy it: International spies, the camera-shy and the generally secretive.

Potential expansion: Like an intestinal parasite, handball is growing rapidly though it's tough to see.

Expect to hear: "Actually, I think you'll find that handball is the fastest growing sport on the planet."

History

Just because Hitler liked something – Shirley Temple movies, vegetarianism, Robert Mugabe-style moustaches – it shouldn't necessarily mean that that thing is inherently wrong. But it's certainly not a bad place to start. Handball was one of Hitler's favourite sports, and was played, by his special request, at the 1936 Olympics. After which the IOC managed to see some sense, dropping it from the competition until 1972, when a, no doubt space-cake fuelled meeting that concluded at 3am led to its inclusion once again. Like a new neighbour who turns up on your doorstep and seems perfectly nice but is a bit too insistent that the two of you are going to be great friends, there's something about handball that doesn't seem quite right. Its history is sketchy to say the least. The first rules of the game were published in 1917 in Germany, the country who also fielded one of the teams at the first international game, presumably made up of players who weren't good enough at football, athletics, winter sports or any of the other sports Germany has seemed to win for as long as anyone has been paying attention. While as far as most people are concerned it remains a minority sport, the governing body – the IHF – maintains that it looks after 159 member federations representing 1,130,000 teams for a total of 31 million players, coaches and officials worldwide. No, really.

You'll Need…

The things you'd need for a game of football. Only smaller. A handball pitch is less than half the size of a football pitch, and a handball ball is about the size of a volleyball, but more tactile and easier to grip. Roller-skating-style knee pads are a good idea. Though why you won't be wearing roller skates is something of a mystery. Once you've equipped the players with protection all you'll need to do is make the ball solid titanium, chuck a couple of motorbikes into the mix and give all the players spiked gauntlets and you'll have a game that really could take the world by storm. You could call it something like 'Deathball 2054'. If the outcome of World War II had been different, then Adolf may well have gone on to adapt his beloved handball into such a sport.

Thrills, action, tension and high drama. All absent in handball.

How You Do It

Continuing with the "like football only smaller" theme, your team of seven has two 30-minute halves to try and score as many goals as possible. Given that even an arthritic pensioner has ten times more control of a ball that's thrown than one that's kicked, handball games tend to be high-scoring affairs. You should be expecting to score after virtually every attack, which makes the whole affair strangely depressing. Like basketball in fact. But at least the big basketball teams have the good sense to populate the court with huge seven-foot freaks of nature to add some human interest to what is basically the schoolgirl's game of netball. Handball is populated by players who are rubbish at everything else and only

handball is left. It's very much the same way as teachers have their careers picked for them.

Advanced

As if to prove it's different from other sports there are a whole bunch of terms for things that happen in the games. If you ever have trouble sleeping, pick up the rules and regulations.

Why You Shouldn't Bother

There's always been a demand for a ball game that's played by teams passing and scoring. It's called football... or hockey or rugby or Aussie rules or volleyball. Handball is to be avoided in football. Or avoided full stop.

Highland Games

The Highland Games have something for everyone, provided you like rupturing yourself while wearing a skirt or dancing on swords.

Country of Origin: Scotland

Possibility of death or serious injury: Only if it's incredibly slippy while dancing on the crossed swords.

Embarrassing clothing: A curious combination of white knee socks, plaid skirt and singlet that makes the hairy-backed wearer look like a grizzly bear at St. Trinian's.

Greatest hazard: A sharp breeze whipping around the Gorbals.

Watch out for: A misdirected caber coming out of the sun... Actually, if the games are taking place in Scotland, there won't be any sun.

Prize/Rewards: The dour Scottish nature is such that the winner can expect nothing more than a reluctant "Aye Hamish, ye didnae do tae bad."

People most likely to enjoy it: Americans who like to fancy they have Scottish heritage because they once ate in McDonald's.

Expect to hear: "Yiz got a problem wiv what I'm werrin?"

History

The Highland Games are as central to Gaelic culture as clan rivalry and stealing cattle. With mass emigration to Canada, America and New Zealand the Scottish diaspora has helped reproduce these games all over the new world with flourishing examples organised and hosted in the Caledonian climates of North

The games regularly attract a colossal bunch of tossers.

Carolina and San Francisco. Only in New Zealand's city of Dunedin can the true miserable wetness of a Scottish summer be adequately reproduced. The games are based on the legend, which has it that Scottish King Malcolm III decided to pick his new messenger by organising a race to the top of Craig Choinnich. The results of this competition are sadly unrecorded, as are Craig's feelings about the small matter of being raced up. But what isn't in doubt is that after getting spanked around the battlefield during a series of Scottish uprisings, the English decided to bend the rules in their favour by banning the training with arms by all men of Scotland. This may go some way to explaining the ferocity of most Scottish women, but more importantly it also explains the origins of the games, as Scotland's disbanded armies looked for ways to maintain their caber tossing and sword dancing prowess. It also led indirectly to a new generation of fearful Scottish weaponry, most notably the bagpipes.

You'll Need...

In the best traditions of the Presbyterian community, organisers will provide pretty much everything you need. Although in keeping with the traditional frugality of the contest, you'll get the sense that a lot of it is being done on the cheap. So while an Olympic competitor will get a shot to put, a Highland Games competitor gets a big stone. And while an Olympics competitor may use a carefully balanced carbon fibre javelin or an ergonomically designed pole-vault pole, a Highland Games competitor will toss a big log.

How You Do It

You do it by being built like Ben Nevis. It's worth pointing out that while a lot of the equipment you'll use looks a lot cruder than traditional athletic equipment, it's also about 40 times heavier. Whatever event you pick. Novice athletes might want to avoid the challenge of tossing a caber and choose a simpler sounding event such as the "weight over the bar". Which sounds easy enough, until you realise the weight amounts to 56 pounds – about the same as an elevator full of supermodels. To shift all that weight you'll need to be carrying a lot of weight yourself and Scottish cuisine is ready to provide that. Scotland is the home of the deep-fried everything, from fush (fish) and chips to pizzas and Mars bars. Whatever foodstuff can survive a battering and a quick immersion into a deep fat fryer, the Scots will eat it, making Glasgow the heart attack capital of Europe. It's no surprise they asked Gordon Ramsay to leave.

Advanced

Many of the games events origins are shrouded in mystery, although the sheaf toss could provide useful practice for any Scottish prime ministers looking to dispose of the details of MP's expense accounts before the public gets hold of them.

Why You Shouldn't Bother

Taking part in the Highland Games is draining, painful and gruelling – and that's just having to listen to the bagpipe rendition of "Scotland the Brave".

Today, the once-noble claymore is the equivalent of a white handbag at a disco. Something to be danced round.

Horse Racing

It's not the sport of kings, it's the sport of midgets. Without a betting element attached, horse racing would be as interesting as a district school sports event without your child involved.

Country of Origin: Unknown
Possibility of death or serious injury: Always high when you perch a malnourished midget atop a couple of tonnes of trampling, snorting horseflesh.
Embarrassing clothing: Although no connection has been made, the shiny jerkins, breeches and funny caps have more than a touch of the gnomish about them. Substitute the fishing rod for a whip and Bob's your uncle.
Watch out for: Suffragettes.
Prize/Rewards: Could be huge, but it doesn't matter, as all jockeys spend their entire working lives unable to think about anything other than a KFC Megabucket or a Burger King meatfeast.
People most likely to enjoy it: Unnaturally small and relatively stupid? This could be the sport for you.
Expect to hear: "Why the long faces?"

History

Horse racing is so old that no one has any idea when it started. We do know that it was practised by the Romans and the Norse. The Romans built fantastic hippodromes, while the Norse invaded the north of England to capture Ripon, York and Wincanton racecourses. Human nature being what it is, we also know that after the completion of the first ever competitive horse race, somebody suggested the riders and their mounts return to the start line to repeat their endeavour, but this time with an extra element added to make things a bit more interesting. And so the first bookies went into business. And as a sport, horse racing has been going downhill ever since.

You'll Need…

To love horses. Well love them enough to enjoy hanging out with them for most of the day, but not so much that you don't mind beating them occasionally as part of your job. Nor so much that you get so attached to them that it cuts

"And moving up on the stand rails it's Meaty Chunks from Woofobix, Dogz Delight and Curry Surprise."

Unlike George Clooney's recent movies, punters love a bet on the grey.

you up when they have to be put out of their misery from the injuries they sustained when you took a jump badly. You'll also need to have no problem being thrown from heights at great speed and getting trampled on regularly. Diet wise you'll need to exist on rations that a supermodel would consider unhealthily small, and without the distraction of chain smoking.

How You Do It

There are two main types of racing – flat racing and National Hunt racing, which has hedge obstacles to jump over – either fences or hurdles. Fences can unseat even the most experienced rider, but it takes a really stupid horse to trip over a hurdle. The most terrifying fences come in the Grand National, which is run at Aintree, near Liverpool, and is generally regarded as the Vietnam of the racing calendar. Not everyone makes it back. Flat racing is racing that takes place on the flat, except at Goodwood in Sussex where they have to lumber up a hill. In fact, such is the steepness of the hill at Goodwood that the last four horses to win there have all used ropes and crampons to get to the top. The good news for horses in Britain is that jockeys are not allowed to raise the whip above their shoulder when they hit them. The bad news for jockeys is that

even though it's physically impossible for horses to get out of their starting stalls, it doesn't stop them trying – scraping the jockey off in the process. So there is a kind of balance.

Advanced

Horse racing is popular across the world, and many of the biggest races have become fixtures in the social calendar. The Kentucky Derby may be considered the most exciting two minutes in sport, but most spectators concentrate on meeting their burgoo and mint julep quotas. In the U.K., the runners and riders at Royal Ascot now get less coverage than common people adopting the traditional upper-class disguise of a stupid hat before blowing their cover by getting drunk on Pimm's. And in Australia the Melbourne Cup is affectionately known as "the race that stops a nation". Though in such a laid-back country it's actually hard to spot the difference.

Why You Shouldn't Bother

Take the betting away and what have you got? Horsey athletics. If you want to gamble, go to Las Vegas. It's more fun and at least they're open about the fact that they've fixed the house odds in their favour.

Ice Hockey

The word "puck" comes from the Irish to poke or deliver a blow, which gives you a linguistic clue as to the real reason anyone watches hockey, or indeed plays it.

Country of Origin: Canada

Possibility of death or serious injury: Every Canadian star from Michael J. Fox to Jacques Villeneuve and Avril Lavigne has their own collection of hockey scars. Serious injury from ice hockey is simply a Canadian rites of passage from youth to adulthood. During a career spanning a decade one professional player spent nine years, 49 weeks and two days encased entirely in plaster.

Embarrassing clothing: Only when you take the padding out and you look like you just made Slimmer of the Year.

Greatest hazard: With razor sharp skates, great big sticks, the puck shooting about the place like a round from a howitzer, it's difficult to single out one hazard as being the greatest.

Watch out for: People who ask you if you'd like to join an ice hockey team. The appropriate response is to move to the safety of a different continent.

Prize/Rewards: Ice hockey players have a great cachet in Canada, but then so does Bryan Adams.

People most likely to enjoy it: Thugs who wear their scars with pride.

Potential expansion: Not with global warming.

Expect to hear: "I think they'll try and ice the puck in the penalty kill."

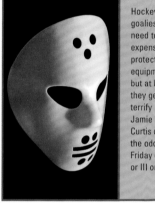

Hockey goalies may need to buy expensive protective equipment, but at least they get to terrify Jamie Lee-Curtis on the odd Friday or II, or III or IV.

History

Older than soccer, cricket and rugby combined, the game of hockey has been played wherever men have been of a mind to knock a ball-like object around on the floor with the aid of a stick-like device for the last four millennia. In between doing each other's eye shadow and walking sideways in the most awkward manner imaginable there's nothing the ancient Egyptians liked more than a game of their own version of field hockey, which like everything else they devised (building the pyramids, carving the Sphinx etc.) was actually executed by slaves. The losing side of which were themselves executed shortly afterwards. The Irish took the sport, made the ball slightly heavier, the sticks a bit broader and the shouting and chanting a lot more guttural. And added alcohol. A lot of alcohol. To be consumed before, during and after the game. This is probably where they got the name for their variation on a classic recipe that became known as hurling. Anyway, it took a mere several hundred years for the citizens of such perpetually icy parts of the planet as Finland and Russia to work out that by flattening the ball a bit, giving the face of the stick a greater surface area and not minding about falling over on their arses a lot they could come up with their very own version of a game that the rest of the civilised world was beginning to realise was a bit of a hit-and-miss affair. Canada hadn't actually been discovered by then, but most Canadians will claim that it's their game in no uncertain terms. And they don't have much else to call their own, so frankly they're welcome to it.

You'll Need…

Padding for every single part of your body, unless you're a goalie, in which case you'll need to rip the armour off a military Humvee to go on every part of your body, plus wear the kind of mask that Michael Crawford should have worn for *Phantom of the Opera*, so that we didn't get to see the grotesque side of his face untouched by the opera house fire.

How You Do It

The good news for people who are about as stable on a pair of ice skates as Amy Winehouse after a minor disagreement with her husband, is that since the 1930s ice hockey has been a game where both forward and backward passes of the puck are allowed. So novices can just skate around hoping that they don't get passed to much and not having to worry about complex manoeuvres such as changing direction. The bad news is that it's a full contact sport. Not only is body checking allowed, it only seems to come, like most things in North America, in a king size, full-fat, high-tar version. With all that padding it's no wonder that sometimes your opponent is a little clumsy and accidentally follows through with his elbow after he's delivered a rib shattering "body check".

Advanced

When playing ice hockey, the best strategy you can employ is to get off the ice as quickly as possible. And the best way to do this, no matter what the bible may say to the contrary, is to meet violence with violence. Not that you'll be looking to do any serious injury of course – just enough so that the referee has no option but to send you to the sin bin. Start by tripping a member of the opposite team with your ergonomically designed stick. That should buy you two minutes out of the game that you'll more than likely double up for delaying the game with your feebly slow attempt to leave the ice. Whatever you do, don't get involved in an actual fight. Ice hockey players are not covered by the Geneva Convention.

Why You Shouldn't Bother

The best thing you can say about ice hockey is that it serves as a vehicle for a bunch of bloodthirsty North Americans to pound the living crap out of each other. All the more reason to leave them to it.

Two players pretend to take an interest in the puck before getting down to the serious business of fighting.

Iditarod

If you veer from the trail during this insane Alaskan dog-sled race there's very little chance that the emergency services will find you in a hurry.

Country of Origin: USA

Possibility of death or serious injury: Serious injury is rare as competitors usually opt for the lonely, frozen death package.

Embarrassing clothing: Will be the last of your worries in extreme weather where the risk of exposure at a toilet stop is more to do with the "dying from" variety than the George Michael kind.

Greatest hazard: The official website says it best…"temperatures far below zero, winds that can cause a complete loss of visibility, the hazards of overflow, long hours of darkness and treacherous climbs and side hills, and you have the Iditarod." Or should that be Idiotrod?

Watch out for: A pack of ravenous dogs deciding that a packet of meaty biscuits isn't quite what they had in mind for their evening meal.

Prize/Rewards: Winners can pocket around $100,000, but you might have to pick up the cheque from Sarah Palin.

People most likely to enjoy it: Those who like to commit suicide in spectacular surroundings.

Expect to hear: "Mush!"

History

Recreating a historic race against time through the frozen wastes to deliver a vital diphtheria serum to Nome, the Iditarod covers a 1,868km course in around nine days. Contestants may experience near-blizzard conditions and must survive hazardous terrain with nothing more than 16 dogs for company. It may not seem the kind of pastime that would appeal to most, but then as anyone who's been there will testify, Alaskans aren't like other folk. As Sarah Palin has now demonstrated. The launch in 1973 of the Iditarod Dog Sled Race was met with general delight from Alaskans, outdoorsmen and explorers everywhere to the utter dismay of the state's canine population. Since then it has firmly established itself as the number one sporting event in the entire state, which is a lot like being the most talented member of the Osbourne family.

You'll Need…

Siberian Huskies are preferred to Alaskan Malamutes – the original sled dog breed. You will need between 12 and 16 of these, along with the amount of food you would expect to give to any creature you're asking to pull you on a sled the distance between Manhattan and Miami in 10 days or less. In a blizzard. While you whip it.

How You Do It

If you're not Alaskan then you should probably focus your efforts not so much on winning the race as surviving to the end of it. However, it's not unknown for non-Alaskans to win it, as the Swiss musher Martin Buser can testify since his 1992 victory, which broke the Alaskan monopoly on the event and proved that the Swiss were good for more than just chocolate, cuckoo clocks and laundering money for the Colombian cartel.

Why You Shouldn't Bother

What else is there to say about a 1,200-mile dog sled race held in the state of America that even most Americans would agree is best seen in your rear view mirror?

Jai Alai

Anything goes in this weird hybrid of squash, tennis and that game you used to play at school when all you had was a tennis ball and a window-free wall.

Country of Origin: Spain

Possibility of death or serious injury: Anything travelling at 150mph is going to sting a bit if it hits you in the face, and goatskin is no exception.

Embarrassing clothing: The kit isn't too bad, but some potential players may balk at the idea of leaping around waving what appears to be a small IKEA wicker banana.

Prize/Rewards: Jai Alai can attract very large wagers and enormous payouts. As a player you'll get none of this.

People most likely to enjoy it: Anyone whose idea of fun is being knocked senseless by a flying goat while holding someone's craft therapy project.

Expect to hear: "Get your dirty hands off my xistera."

History

Named after one of the merry festivals at which it would have been played, Jai Alai comes to us from the Basque region in Northern Spain, groaning under the weight of expectations you'd naturally expect of any game that claims to be the fastest on Earth. The city of Miami has become Jai Alai's spiritual U.S. home, although like most things America realises it doesn't need, it was exported to Mexico, where the first court opened in 1928, giving Mexicans yet another reason to feel aggrieved.

You'll Need...

A ball – called a pelota – which has to be fashioned from the skin of one of the planet's fastest moving creatures, the…goat. More importantly, you'll need a two-foot-long glove made of wicker and called a xistera.

How You Do It

Like Colombian hitmen, Jai Alai players work in pairs, with up to eight teams contesting any given match in a format where the winner stays on after each round. So it's a bit like playing pool in the pub, except the challenging team aren't required to pay for a new set of balls. With the court surface marked out in parallel lines you may feel as if you're standing in a giant exercise book. A successful serve will land between lines 4 and 7, after that it's anyone's guess what is supposed to happen, though presumably being knocked unconscious is the ultimate aim.

Why You Shouldn't Bother

Jai Alai draws its players from an established pool of talent in South America and Miami, both places where an ability to avoid getting hit by speeding projectiles is a highly valued skill. And like organised crime, it's definitely something that's best left to the professionals.

Can also be used as a lampshade.

Javelin

Stick some Ancient Olympic competitors in a time machine and transport them to the modern games and they'd find it difficult to recognise the synchronised swimming or the beach volleyball. But they would recognise the javelin...

Country of Origin: Greece

Possibility of death or serious injury: Yes, there is always the potential of scoring a personal worst, i.e. slipping during your run-up and embedding the thing in your ear. Though tragic, this would give a big comedy moment to the other people waiting in Accident and Emergency... and at least they wouldn't have to say, "what are you in for...?"

Embarrassing clothing: The days of competitors being naked and oiled are over. And thankfully they were over long before Fatima Whitbread took up the sport.

Greatest hazard: Having a flashback to Thermopylae and taking out the Jamaican relay team.

Watch out for: The guys with the tape measure.

Prize/Rewards: Medals, plus the certain knowledge that if NATO were to go green and de-spec the armed forces, then you'd be first in line for your own troop of javelin throwers.

Expect to hear: "Heads up!"

History

It'll come as no surprise to most people to learn that the Ancient Olympics were markedly different from the Olympic Games as we know them today. For one thing, all competitors had to be male, free citizens and Greek speaking. The games were always hosted in Olympia – not the conference centre in London, but a town in the West Grecian province of Ilia. Yet despite the many differences between the ancient and modern games, there still remain strong threads that connect the modern day, media-saturated, multi-billion-dollar extravaganzas with a bunch of off-duty Greek soldiers frolicking about, probably naked. Several events remain in many ways unchanged from the kind of sporting activities those de-mob-happy lads probably got up to, and key among them is the javelin. The act of being able to chuck a spear a good distance would have been one that was highly prized by the various ancients, Greeks, Trojans, Goths and Emos alike. And you can bet that had they assembled for the javelin tournament, the same thought would have gone through the collective minds of the ancient spectators as goes through that of the modern viewing audience today. Namely, why is it that the thing never ends up stuck satisfyingly in the ground?

You'll Need...

A javelin. The modern 800g male javelin was redesigned and standardised in 1984 because the East Germans had got so good at it they were putting holes in the running track. The redesign shifted the centre of gravity to give it a more downward pitch and reduce the flight distance by around 10 per cent. After a lengthy consultation process and several redesigns, colour changes and minor alterations, the 600g women's javelin was given a similar makeover, by which time most female athletes had decided they actually probably preferred it as it was. In any case, the new javelins did now at least land in the stadium that they'd been thrown in.

So far the IAAF have resisted calls to liven up the javelin with animal targets and a 30m dartboard.

How You Do It

Unlike other Olympic throwing events, javelineers get a run-up, and this is key to achieving a successful throw. Competitors should ensure that they remain on their own side of the throwing line for two reasons. Firstly, if they cross the line by so much as a centimetre during their throw, that throw will not be counted. Secondly, and most importantly, the kind of injuries pictured here have only ever happened to unfortunates on the other side of the line. Interesting to note that whilst it rarely stays stuck in the ground, the modern javelin seems to have no trouble firmly embedding itself in human flesh. The current world record for the javelin is 98.48m, a throw made in 1996 by Jan Železný. Sadly, sports fans, you can't quite make out on YouTube whether it stayed in the ground or not.

Why You Shouldn't Bother

The prestigious garland of World's Greatest Athlete is traditionally afforded to the Olympic champion in the decathlon – a gruelling event comprising 10 different disciplines ranging from the pole vault to the 100m to the 1500m. So if you're Olympic champion Roman Šebrle, you're going to be light on your feet. In 2007 Šebrle was training in South Africa when he was hit by a javelin thrown by a female athlete and was a pencil's length from being hit in the throat or heart. Which just goes to show how dangerous a javelin can be. Even when it's thrown by a girl.

Judo

Judo is a fighting style that focuses almost exclusively on that section of the conflict where combatants grab each other's clothes, so the right attire is key. The key factor is a robustly constructed quilted body with an easily grabbable lapel.

Country of Origin: Japan

Possibility of death or serious injury: This is a sport that most closely resembles ballroom dancing with extra laying down and wiggling. Unsurprisingly, survival rates are high.

Embarrassing clothing: Not really. Most teenagers are quite happy to wander around in pyjamas all day and if you adore white, or slightly off-white, then you'll be more than happy.

Greatest hazard: Falling asleep during a protracted "hold".

Prize/Rewards: If you're talented and focused enough to reach the highest echelons of the judo world, you'll find you've acquired an amazing collection of coloured belts. So you'll never go short of a curtain tie.

People most likely to enjoy it: Worth considering if you like the idea of being a kickboxer, but aren't sure about being kicked.

Expect to hear: "I think he went for a quick ashigirami."

History

Devotees of judo are drawn by its "gentle way" – a belief that an opponent may be defeated through the application of force indirectly. As such it has gained a reputation for being the most feminine of the martial arts, in keeping with other forms of achieving objectives by indirect means such as: the silent treatment, withholding sexual favours and threatening to invite your parents over for the weekend of the cup final. Invented in the later part of the nineteenth century by Kano Jigoro, a frail and physically puny specimen who was tired of getting sand kicked in his face at the beach, judo was designed to be more than just a fighting system, and ideally would become an holistic system for life improvement that could lead its practitioners into "mutual prosperity". Presumably once they'd finished chucking around and half strangling each other.

You'll Need...

A white robed affair as favoured by medical orderlies, beauty therapists and Luke Skywalker. You'll also need someone larger than you to fight. Judo is the martial art where the essential skill is using your opponent's weight against them, the heavier the better, although sadly if you're lucky enough to find someone who's into avoiding trips to the salad bar and also into martial arts, chances are they're a practising sumo.

How You Do It

All bouts start with a ceremonial bow to your opponent called a rei. This is done to show your respect for the opponent you have every intention of humiliating in about 10 seconds' time. Once this pantomime of supposed good karma is out of the way the two judoka can move onto the combat, which happens in two distinct phases. In the standing phase the two combatants will attempt to throw each other, ideally with one of those neat moves so beloved of spy movies and kids' TV dramas. This almost never happens, and the standing phase tends to consist of the two fighters dragging each other around the dojo by the lapels, like two drunks in a pub car park, until either one or both of them is tripped, spun, or just plain falls over. Since whoever falls is hanging onto those lapels for dear life, both judoka end up on the floor, ready for phase two – the ground phase. This resembles nothing more than two inexperienced lovers attempting an advanced position from the karma sutra. Sadly their lack of form in this department shows in the fact that neither of them has removed their pyjamas. A lot of red-faced grunting ensues until the referee has decided he's had enough.

Advanced

While devotees of Judo claim that rank is of no importance, clearly it is. Why else would they choose to walk around wearing a belt that displays their supposed ability to pin you to the ground and make you say things about your own mother you could never repeat? Still, gradings tend to be less scary than you'd expect and if you stick around in the same club for long enough you might make it to yellow in a couple of years on sympathy alone.

Why You Shouldn't Bother

Kano Jigoro intended Judo to be more than just a sport – he wanted it to be a way of life and a means of self defence too. Which it could be, as long as you're lucky enough to run into a mugger wearing something with a thick, strong, easy-grip lapel, which he doesn't mind you grabbing hold of. And he isn't carrying a knife.

One of only three successful throws executed in 2008.

Kabbadi

For every action there is an equal and opposite reaction. For every ying there is a yang. For Australian rules football there is Kabbadi.

Country of Origin: India

Possibility of death or serious injury: Hold your breath too long and you may faint, but should that happen you can always count on your hand-holding buddies to give you the kiss of life. Probably for several hours after you've recovered.

Embarrassing clothing: Any sport that requires the wearing of pants and just pants is to be avoided.

People most likely to enjoy it: If your idea of a well-spent Saturday afternoon is two 20-minute bouts of sweaty, near-naked hand-holding then you'd probably be better off just having sex.

Potential expansion: With just minor adjustments the sport could really take off as Kabuggery.

Expect to hear: "Kabbadi, Kabbadi, Kabbadi, Kabbadi etc..."

History

Even the most seasoned of travellers admit that there's something about the Indian experience which puts it in a different league from other destinations. It may be the fact that, while technically a country, India is both populous and diverse enough to feel like an entire continent. It might be the contrast between the friendly and generous nature of the people with the confrontational and aggressive nature of the cuisine. Or maybe it's the fact that the world's most risk-taking, horn-blowing, breaking-the-speed-limit-as-a-matter of-course drivers are to be found sharing their roads with wild monkeys, wilder children and cows that have become so used to their sacred

status that they've actually started to believe their own press and think that they're invincible. But somewhere in the cultural kaleidoscope that travellers to India experience, one of the stranger things has to be the game of Kabbadi, a sport where holding hands is as important an element as holding your breath (Kabbadi means holding breath), played by grown men. In their pants.

You'll Need...

A mere seven buddies to make up your team. Players should have no problem being seen in public holding hands with other moustachioed men. Also, a pair of generously sized coloured underpants that makes you look like a beach bum from a 1950s Hollywood film, such as *From Here to Eternity*.

How You Do It

A game of Kabbadi takes place over two 20-minute halves. Teams take turns to send one of their number – a raider – across to the other team, which for that round are defending. The raider has to attempt to break the defending team's chain. While holding his breath. Possibly chanting the word Kabbadi. The defending team have to try and confine him and stop him from returning to his own side before he draws a breath. The defending team don't have to hold their breath or chant anything, although there's nothing in the rules to stop them from doing so. And in the grand tradition of administration learnt from the British, but perfected by India, there are six officials – a referee, two umpires, a scorer and two assistant scorers. Plans to extend this number to include two assistant umpires and an official to provide chai at half-time are currently being reviewed by several committees of officials from a dedicated wing

The slogan on the pants reads: "May God guide my most splendid efforts in Kabbadi and let my opponents feel the glorious thunder of my thighs upon their unworthy skins."

of the Asian Kabbadi Federation's Special Administrative Task Force. And their assistants.

Advanced

Of course, like everything else in India, there's incredible variety depending on what region of the country you're in, so as with parking restrictions or just how spicy "very spicy" means on the menu, don't be surprised if wherever you go the rules seem to change.

Why You Shouldn't Bother

A typical round of Kabbadi goes something like this. Two groups of seven men square up to each other, and the most aggressive of one group leaves the pack and advances alone towards the defenders, muttering something to himself. He seems to set his sights on the smallest member of the defending team. While the defenders outnumber him, they are wary, and stand by their team mate in a show of support. There's a bit of a kerfuffle, but no punches are thrown, and try as they might to stop him, the attacker manages to get away and make it back to his own group. It's remarkable for a country that places such a high value on sobriety that Kabbadi so closely resembles a skirmish in a busy pub car park on Friday night. All that's missing are a couple of shouts of "Forget it, it's not worth it!" And a kebab shop nearby.

Kendo

If the unpredictability, danger and sheer excitement of fencing seems like it might be too much for you, why not try a sport where you have to tell your opponent where you're going to try and hit them before you try and hit them?

Country of Origin: Japan

Possibility of death or serious injury: Small. In an effort to promote safety and accuracy, the legitimate "hit" areas on your opponent's body are limited to spaces only a few microns wide.

Embarrassing clothing: Extremely. Prepare yourself to look like the bastard child of a medieval monk and a cheap disposable barbeque.

Watch out for: Embarrassing mix-ups with Kandoo, the flushable wipe for toilet training kids.

People most likely to enjoy it: Those who believe that spiritual and mental perfection can be achieved by dressing up like a *Dr Who* monster, bashing people with a stick and shouting.

Potential expansion: Outside of Japan the sport mainly seems to appeal to people who call themselves Darth Paul and make vvvwummmm noises when they wave their bamboo stick around.

Expect to hear: "Men! Kote! Do! Tsuki! Ra Ra Ra!" and stuff.

---

ancient art of samurai swordplay relates to two blokes in bathrobes swinging cast-offs from a garden centre and shouting a lot, no one seems able to say. Kendo has claims to have an international following, being practised by just over eight million people worldwide, eight million of whom live in Japan. These numbers have grown rapidly since the eighteenth century when the introduction of the aforementioned bamboo training sword allowed exponents of the art to vastly increase their chances of leaving the sporting arena with a full complement of limbs, albeit with a commensurate loss of dignity.

You'll Need...

Traditional martial arts robes, as many parents will testify, are extremely expensive and the cause of as many arguments as the tidiness of rooms and appropriateness of attire in many a teenage home. So unless you fancy gambling the cost of the kit on the remote chance that you'll actually want to attempt kendo more than once, make do with the largest dressing

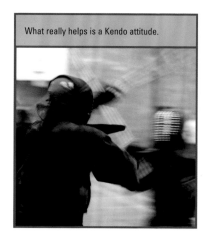

What really helps is a Kendo attitude.

History

A little island that has punched above its weight commercially, culturally and militarily throughout its history, Japan's greatest gift to the world after sushi, porno mag vending machines and tamagotchis would without doubt be the martial arts. Of these, Kendo probably has the strongest links to its origins in samurai training – Kendo literally translates as "way of the sword". Though quite how the

gown you can lay hands on. A simple household sieve secured with the elastic bands left by the postman will be ideal for a mask. If your instructor questions you on your appearance tell him that your other robes are in the wash.

How You Do It

Many novices are surprised to discover the strong connection that exists between a violent, confrontational and above all noisy sport like Kendo, and the spiritual path of Zen Buddhism. For the samurai, knowing one's place in the universe was central to attaining wisdom. In real terms this meant knowing that the samurai's life meant nothing other than to be given in the name of his emperor. Being convinced that the outcome of any violent encounter and even the loss of one's own life were inconsequential in the grand scheme of things made the samurai a fearsome opponent. However, the disdain for the outcome of an individual bout had the potential to turn Kendo into the most boring spectator sport ever as the two combatants, knowing that the result of their combat was of total insignificance to the universe, instead downed their weapons and composed haikus about butterflies. For this reason the IOC introduced a scoring system that has been adopted by Kendo schools worldwide, where combatants score points for successful strikes, thrusts at specified areas, and having the scariest shout. Unusually it is necessary for participants to state the strike zone which they are targeting, and they are only awarded points if their specified target matches where they land a blow. So there are no lucky hits in Kendo, a practice which, were it applied to other sports, would probably deny Manchester United the last six trophies they've won and prevent them from winning ever again.

Advanced

Whilst Japanese culture can seem somewhat alien to a westerner, the concept of Mushin – having an empty mind – is one that can be instantly adopted by anyone in Australia or the U.K. simply by watching an episode of *Neighbours*.

Why You Shouldn't Bother

Despite its scary and shouty image, Kendo is actually the most polite of all the martial arts. And also the one that most resembles two people doing a rather angry version of the hokey-cokey.

Kendo is 65 per cent dressing up, 20 per cent shouting, 10 per cent interior decoration and 5 per cent martial art. Having signalled where you are about to strike, the only real surprise is if you shout in a sarcastic accent.

Kinetic Sculpture Racing

A sport devised by hippies for hippies, which means it's not about the winning, it's about the taking part and expressing yourself in an astrally balanced way.

Country of Origin: USA

Possibility of death or serious injury: Medically, it is possible for people to die of shame. Why no kinetic sculpture racer has yet done so is testament to the level of self-delusion in hippies.

Embarrassing clothing: As an integral part of your travelling artwork you will be expected to look like a complete and utter w**ker. But as we are talking about the contemporary art world here – which is made up almost entirely of complete and utter w**kers – it'll be hard to attract enough attention to be embarrassed.

Greatest hazard: Any kind of breakdown may not only leave you stranded but disqualified on the grounds of not being kinetic any more.

Watch out for: Kinetic "artworks" that are about as artistic as Tracy Emin's tent.

People most likely to enjoy it: Self-proclaimed "craaaazy guys".

Potential expansion: Some critics have suggested that KSR is only the start of putting modern art to some tangible sporting use. Another would be to get the entire contents of Tate Modern and concrete them into an installation called "Foundations of an Olympic Stadium".

Expect to hear: "Like, wow, your two-man swordfish is smokin', dude!"

History

If you were able to cross a carnival float with a triathlon race, then kinetic sculpture racing would be the bastard offspring. Though as the whole concept is hippie-inspired, then "lovechild" is probably a more appropriate term. Think of it as a birdman competition where the entrants have to race a modern work of art which won't fall apart 10 metres beyond the startline.

You'll Need...

A human-powered, all-terrain, amphibious work of art. Seriously. Until recently the birdman competitions of Europe and the weekly Zoobomb event in Portland, Oregon pretty much had the monopoly on weird vehicles, but kinetic sculpture racing seems to be proclaiming itself the Captain Beefheart of the sports world in its possibly inspired but almost certainly deranged attempts to be the craziest kid on the block.

How You Do It

There are several competitions spread across the USA, and each has its own particular take on what constitutes a kinetic sculpture. But since all the events are run by hippies you shouldn't worry about the rules too much. Essentially you'll be taking a bike, tricycle or other pedal powered machine and making it – and yourself – as weird looking as you can. If you're not blessed with much of an imagination that might just mean adorning it with the Kinetic chicken logo adopted by the original

A kinetic sculpture racing machine at Boulder, Colorado. Damien Hirst offered to create all the machines for the 2009 event, but organisers couldn't afford the $192m price tag.

event in Humboldt County California, putting clown rouge on your cheeks, and wearing a silly hat. That's the most important part of the event handled, and as you can see, entrants don't tend to pull any punches in their aim to be the most outrageous. Once you've prepared your vehicle you'll be ready to tackle the course itself, which in the case of the original event is remarkably hardcore considering the whole deal is aimed at artistic types, stretching as it does over 41 miles of river, road, dune and gut-churning drops.

Advanced

There's an uneasy trade-off between artistic merit and built-for-speed practicality and many of the early exponents are calling for an artistic threshold that each entrant should meet. Is the piece challenging enough to take part or is it just a go-kart with a glass-fibre chicken strapped to it? KSR also provides a family friendly, not-for-profit, carbon neutral distraction for an audience of confused but mildly amused passers by. What's more worrying is that the rise of events across the USA and now the emergence of events in

places as far away as Geraldton, Western Australia proves that hippie lunacy can no longer be put down to local meteorological conditions in the state of California, and is growing on enough of a scale to classify it as an international epidemic. It's believed to have spread to backwoods communities of rural Kentucky where teams of brothers, sisters and cousins compete in kinfolk sculpture racing.

Why You Shouldn't Bother

Many contestants will be lured in by the spirit of these events, and possibly by the fact that however useless your contraption and your ability to complete the course, there'll probably be an award for you, from "worst prepared team" to "best bribe" and "most amusing mechanical breakdown involving the loss of a limb". Entering one of these races may seem like a great idea at 3.30am on the back of a bong or eight. But like the idea of asking that homeless guy down the road if he wants to crash on your couch till he gets himself together, or having the word "rainbow" tattooed across your forehead, it's one that you'd be wise to dismiss in the cold light of day.

Kite Surfing

With so many ways to get seriously injured or die while kite surfing, there is some consolation in the knowledge that it will take a very fast and persevering shark to catch you. Unless you fall off. Which you will.

Country of Origin: China

Possibility of death or serious injury: If you're the kind of namby pamby, limp-wristed panty waister who's going to complain when what remains of your bloated, shark-chewed body is dragged out of the ocean by a passing oil tanker six weeks later then you shouldn't bother.

Embarrassing clothing: No. Survival takes priority.

Greatest hazard: If your kite comes down eight miles out to sea it can be quite difficult running up and down to get it aloft again.

Prize/Rewards: The adrenalin thrill of any great extreme sport coupled with the extra rush of being carried out into the Pacific with night closing in and your loud "baggies" offering the only chance of being spotted by rescue helicopters.

People most likely to enjoy it: Surfers, kayak paddlers, hang-glider pilots, thrill-seeking flying fish who want to extend their glide time.

Expect to hear: "I was getting some serious air but then my donkey dick snapped off."

A kite surfer sets out from Australia's Gold Coast. Next stop, Hawaii.

History

Along with the invention of fireworks, Indian ink and toilet paper, the Chinese are credited with being the first people on the planet to use the kite as a means of propulsion. As far back as the thirteenth century the wise men of the Orient experimented with a variety of ways to harness the incredible power of the wind to fuel a mode of personal transport. Finding that there was no way to make such a device controllable they very sensibly abandoned the notion and stuck to using the wind to send their ships across oceans, grind the grain in their mills, and dry their washing on laundry day. Eight hundred years later, a golden generation of design and watersport enthusiasts from all over the world have developed kite propulsion to such a fine degree that you can now go kitesurfing, kite landboarding, kite buggying, kite skateboarding and snowkiting... and all with the same degree of control as NASA landing a rogue satellite.

You'll Need...

Quite a bit of gear, as it turns out – kite, board, harness, lines and bar to hang on to for dear life, for starters. You might also want to invest in a wetsuit to slightly postpone the onset of hypothermia, and a GPS tracking device would be a nice thought as it would at least give the Air-Sea rescue helicopter a headstart over the sharks.

How You Do It

Any Charlie Browner will tell you that this sport is not one you can learn from a book – it's something you can only advance in if you get out there and try a few moves. To start off you'll need to see how adept you are at flying a kite on a beach, then move on to the *CSI*-sounding "body-dragging" where you romp into the surf and let the kite drag you around for an hour or two.

If you're a novice you might want to take dawn patrol as it won't be so jammed and is less likely to be nuking. A bit of tea-bagging is inevitable at first, but if you want to avoid proper kitemares like Hindenberging or taking a dookie dive then don't head out in *Victory at Sea* conditions. Oh, and learning kite boarding lingo is essential too.

Advanced

"Controlled flying" is described as one of the biggest attractions of the sport, but with the reminder that it is "difficult and dangerous". As if being suddenly dragged into the air by an unpredictable force was going to be "quite simple and mildly diverting". A pointer as to just *how* difficult and dangerous is given by one of the guys that helped develop the sport in the 1990s. Hawaiian Laird Hamilton is the man who helped introduce tow-surfing to the world – where a surfer is towed by a jetski into the path of monster 50- and 60-foot waves that they couldn't paddle into by hand.

Why You Shouldn't Bother

Anyone who was freaked out by the Winnie the Pooh story where Pooh gets carried off by a balloon will be predisposed to avoid kite surfing. When demonstrated by experts it looks a fantastic thrill ride. What people forget is that each beginner swallows his/her own weight in sea water for the first six months of learning. With speeds of 50 knots-plus possible and every chance that you'll be dragged out to sea – or on a very gusty day into the flight path of a 747 – it's little wonder that this sport attracts a hardcore audience.

Sharks find kite surfers particularly annoying. One minute they've got dinner all lined up, the next...

Lacrosse

Lacrosse is one of the magnificent gifts of the Native American people to Western culture, along with scalping, smoke signals, teepees and the Cherokee Indian from the Village People.

Country of Origin: North America

Possibility of death or serious injury: By the end of a game you should expect to feel in a similar condition to the morning after a night drinking tequila, but without the sense that you've had any kind of fun.

Embarrassing clothing: In the women's game, short skirts and large knickers are worn. It has been suggested that the game might improve its popularity if this was changed to just a short skirt.

Watch out for: Overdeveloped thighs.

Prize/Rewards: An instant camaraderie with anybody else who was made to play the sport as a child and who has the scars to prove it.

People most likely to enjoy it: Sturdy girls with loud, braying voices.

Potential expansion: After 300 years you'd have thought that if lacrosse were going to catch on in a big way it would have done so by now.

Expect to hear: "Lacrosse players do it with a weird bit of webbing."

History

If Lacrosse had a golden age then it was surely the 1700s when it became popular in the newly founded colonies of America, particularly New England where it rapidly became the second most popular pastime after witch hunting. The rules of the game owe their roots to a tournament used by Native Americans as a means of settling conflicts between individuals or groups without them having to resort to violence. In its Native American form games would last from dawn to dusk, with contestants frequently collapsing in exhaustion at the end of a day's play and waking only to have to start all over again where they left off. This alone is a great reason not to play it in its original form, but it does make it a great game for your kids to play during the long summer holidays. Ideally in someone else's garden.

You'll Need...

Wherever you look in this strange hybrid of hockey, handball and egg-and-spoon racing you come across religious imagery. The name

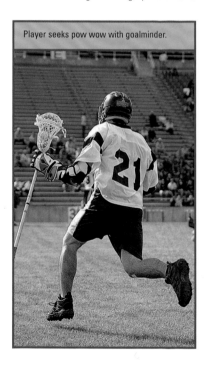
Player seeks pow wow with goalminder.

allegedly comes from the resemblance of the stick to a bishop's crozier. If the church has anything to do with this form of ritual savagery then it's about time they apologised for it in the same way that they apologised for the Spanish Inquisition. In any case, you'll need one rubber ball to play plus a stick for every team member. These come in two lengths, "short" being just over a metre in length and "long" being just under two metres. Though, as the female members on your team will no doubt point out, it doesn't matter how long it is if you don't know what to do with it. Which you won't.

How You Do It

Despite its St. Trinians/girls boarding school image, lacrosse actually can get pretty nasty at times and certainly revels in its full contact status. Aside from the battering you'll get from the body checking, there's a ball you need to avoid, or, failing that, chase after. This is generally scooped up and carried in the cross at around face height. On a positive note, the old Native American practice of using a rock has been replaced by something slightly less robust. So when you get hit by the rubber ball

travelling at 100mph you can reassure yourself that any damage done is probably only likely to be semi-permanent.

Advanced

One of the reasons that the sport may have died out amongst the Native American communities is that in its original form it was often played by teams of anything between 100 and 1,000 men. And after a few years of less than amicable dealings with their newly arrived European neighbours the Native Americans would have struggled to get two teams out. And while there is a Native American team sanctioned to play internationally, it remains a sport that's only got a local following. The 2004 European Championships were attended by a mere seven nations.

Why You Shouldn't Bother

Lacrosse shares the category of handball as a sport which is really struggling for market share. Most people only play it because they're made to play it – like Scrabble with your relations at Christmas.

North American kids do it with helmets, protective pads and gloves. English boarding school girls do it with little or no protection. And half the lads from the local village.

Luge

Put simply, the luge is toboganning for perverts. Take one small sledge, take one rubber fetishist with a love of the cold and put them together on an icy alpine track and you have – the luge.

Country of Origin: Switzerland

Possibility of death or serious injury: Yes, and often in front of the world's media.

Embarrassing clothing: Yes – oh yes, yes, yes. The luge is a must for anyone comfortable in a gimp costume and shiny helmet. Not only that, they wear the most ridiculous "speed slippers" that even self-respecting male ballet dancers would turn their noses up at.

Watch out for: "…the next turn!"

Prize/Rewards: The thrill of wearing rubber in a public place – at speed.

People most likely to enjoy it: Germans with small moustaches.

Potential expansion: Lugeing at home. It couldn't be simpler. Order a massive poster of a snowy alpine scene and glue it to the ceiling of your utility room. Dress up in your luge suit (if you haven't got one, Anne Summers do a very close alternative). Get some ice cubes from the fridge. Place your luge on top of the washing machine and switch it to fast spin. Mount your luge on top while scattering ice cubes down your suit. Wait for the spin cycle to stop, then dismount and wave to the crowd.

Expect to hear: "Fritz, what's that poking in my back?"

History

Swiss hotelier Capser Badrutt aided by a bunch of Victorian English gentlemen were responsible for a great number of winter sports. Badrutt owned a spa hotel in St Moritz and was fed up catering for guests only in the short summer season. So he challenged some English regulars to a bet: he would give them winter lodging for free if they found the locale inhospitable and dull on a lengthy winter stay, and if he won their satisfaction, they had to talk up the experience amongst their acquaintances. The five gentlemen were well connected, travelling in wealthy circles, and almost overnight wintering in St Moritz at Badrutt's hotel became the rage. Searching out diversions, a few Englishmen adapted a child's delivery sled for daring dashes down the twisting narrow streets. Subsequently, their wives wanted a Victorian ride, and larger steerable devices were contrived – respectively the early Luge/Skeleton individual sleds and the Bobsled (or Bobsleigh). Careening around the town's streets was good fun, but

Apart from the speed slippers, lugers have to wear a helmet than makes them look like a penis when standing up.

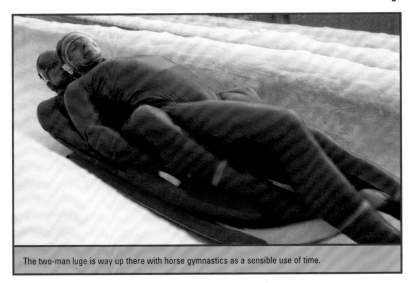

The two-man luge is way up there with horse gymnastics as a sensible use of time.

the incidence and frequency of pedestrian collisions and risk to life and limb grew proportionately. So Badrutt stepped in and built the first half-pipe track.

You'll Need…

A luge. This is in essence a small one- or two-person sled with flexible runners which the pilot controls by a combination of calf and shoulder movement. For practical purposes it looks little different from the kind of basic delivery boy sled that kicked off the whole winter sports deal in the late 1800s. You'll also need a track. Most of these are artificial, kept icy by means of refrigeration. So-called natural tracks are about as natural as Dolly Parton's figure, though almost as curvy to give them their due. A full list of tracks can be obtained from the sport's governing body – the FIL – which is based in Germany and whose executive committee is dominated by Germans. This might explain the sports ongoing unpopularity.

How You Do It

The position you adopt on the luge is supine – feet first, flat on your back. This is considered an excellent position for the human body as it allows the vertebrae of the back to fully extend and relax. All of which is utterly irrelevant for anyone on the luge, since it's nearly impossible to relax when you're balanced on a tea tray hurtling towards the unknown at speeds of up to 80mph. The position your body will actually be in will closely resemble that of an eight-year-old spending their first night in bed alone without a night light – flat on your back but so rigid with fear it's all you can do to peer down towards the foot of the bed as you try to work out just what kind of monster it was that made the noise you heard.

Advanced

In competition, riders compete against the clock, and track deterioration is a big factor. Though frankly the track's deterioration will be nothing compared to that of your reputation should you be photographed taking part in a doubles event. The men's double luge remains without doubt the biggest excuse for a simulated act of buggery ever devised, beating even the snap in American football.

Why You Shouldn't Bother

If you're really determined to head down a bobsleigh run on something you'd find in someone's kitchen, do it in a wok. Woks are really immensely practical, and wok racing is on the rise. IKEA sell them at knock-down prices. No one uses tea trays any more.

Can you spot the Tour de France rider who's taken the most drugs...?

Lumberjack Sports

They're furry, they race up trees panting, they chop down trees and then they put trees in the river and roll them round and round. No, not beavers, we're talking about loggers. And guess what they like to do in their leisure hours...?

Country of Origin: Canada

Possibility of death or serious injury: It's no different from everyday lumberjacking. So very likely indeed.

Embarrassing clothing: Not at all. In some places lumberjack wear is considered very fashionable. Canadian lesbian bars for example.

Greatest hazard: As hazards go, being struck on the head by a large tree obeying the laws of gravity scores highly on the "certain death" table.

Watch out for: Beards so big you'll think the new trend in Islamic fundamentalism is to wear plaid and Timberlands.

History

The lumberjack's role in the history of North America is a proud one that's been celebrated in the literature of Ken Kesey and the songs of Monty Python. And while the improvements in technology have made the job of logging safer, quicker and a whole lot noisier, there remains a strong pull for many to the old bunkhouse traditions of old. Whether or not the lumberjack nostalgia industry has got its history right or not, there's clearly an audience for this kind of tosh. The Lumberjack World Championship has been held in Wisconsin every year since 1960 and generally attracts an audience of something like 12,000 people. Though given that the audience tends to comprise someone's dad, a stressed mom and at least three bored kids, it's unlikely that any more than a fifth of that audience has actually chosen to be there.

You'll Need...

Lumberjack clobber. LJ sports share a great deal with the Scottish highland games. Indeed, on a surface level the biggest difference would seem to be that while the Scots choose to compete in skirts, the Canadians do not, preferring to wear macho checked shirts, spiked boots called caulks and jeans with wide braces over their lace bras.

How You Do It

Competitors chop wood, saw wood and climb up trees, sometimes simultaneously. But the event which has done most to capture the imaginations of viewing audiences across Wisconsin is log rolling or birling – which puts two contestants on a floating log, where the object is to spin the log, forcing your opponent to lose his balance while maintaining your own. Many think the addition of 20" chainsaws would take this to a new level.

These competitors were later disqualified for not having beards.

Marathon Running

Marathon runners often talk of hitting "the wall" when their bodies run out of glycogen. Experienced runners will encounter this wall at around the 20-mile point and first timers shortly before they cross the start line.

Country of Origin: Greece

Possibility of death or serious injury: Sadly, a number of runners each year suffer heart attacks related to the physical stress of running nearly 30 miles. Which just goes to show that smoking 40 cigarettes a day can be the healthy option.

Embarrassing clothing: Good quality running shoes, a pair of shorts that won't chafe and a singlet are all you'll need. Oh and a full gorilla costume.

Watch out for: Z-list celebrities running past TV cameras looking increasingly knackered.

Prize/Rewards: Everyone gets a free sheet of tinfoil at the finish line, plus a *Jim'll Fix It*-style medal that looks like it's come from The Pound Shop.

People most likely to enjoy it: The charitably well-intentioned and the insane.

Expect to hear: "I'm expecting it to be renamed Snickers."

History

We all know the story of Pheidippides, the Greek soldier sent from the battle of Marathon back to the Greek Senate to communicate news of another famous victory. Known amongst his colleagues in the messaging department as "a bit of a management suck-up" he took his responsibilities so seriously that he completed his mission without taking his Union-negotiated mandatory break and as a result dropped dead of a heart attack the second he finished reciting his message. A message that amounted to telling the top brass "We won" – a message of about as much strategic importance as revealing what colour underwear Plutarch was wearing that day.

You'll Need...

Six months of your life to devote to training. Methods vary but essentially there are two phases to a training programme, "building" and "tapering". During the "building" phase athletes will run every other day, building up the distance covered on each training run by around 10 per cent a week, up to and sometimes beyond the distance covered in an actual marathon. The "tapering" phase will usually start in the fortnight before the event, and during this time runners will cover shorter distances and give their bodies the chance to recover before the big day. In recent years

An iconic London marathon view – runners crossing Tower Bridge. They should open it just a little.

Using time-lapse photography, marathon runners are shown shuffling from left to right.

many inexperienced runners have chosen to reduce the "building" phase of their training and focus more on the "tapering". On the day of the race itself these runners are usually said to be "well and truly f***ed".

How You Do It

The key to marathon running is to set off at a manageable pace that can be maintained for the entire distance. It's also vital to avoid injury both during training and on the day itself. Good foot care and running shoes that fit properly are vital, as even minor irritations can escalate over such a distance. Runners who experience nagging annoyances during the race will understand how their friends have felt over the last six months of being regaled with training programme stories and constant pestering for sponsorship.

Advanced

At the top of the sport little has changed since the days of Pheidippides, with runners opting out of the opportunity to relieve themselves at

appropriate locations and simply dumping in the street. Not something that's generally encouraged, but next time you get asked by a police officer what the hell you think you're doing pissing against a lamppost on Friday night you could always offer the excuse that you're in training for a marathon.

Why You Shouldn't Bother

Marathon runners have the kind of pseudo religious zeal that makes non-marathon runners uneasy. Some take part in one marathon and rightly say "never again"; it's the ones that get the gleam in their eye and say "maybe I could do Paris next year" that you have to watch. Whether or not marathon running does us any good is a matter of ongoing debate, as despite extensive research wildly differing opinions exist as to where the endurance limits of the human body are. What seems clear is that if either God or evolution wanted us to run 26.2 miles without stopping, we'd have toenails that didn't turn black and drop off after covering such distances.

Mini Golf

Mini or Crazy Golf is the sport of choice for the mentally challenged or the presidentially suitable. It might be better termed "Crap Golf".

Country of Origin: USA

Possibility of death or serious injury: Low, though by the third hole you might wish it were otherwise.

Watch out for: People whose job involves sitting in a tiny shed handing out clubs and balls all day. Interestingly, these are proven to be the surliest humans in all of creation.

Prize/Rewards: A hearty dose of existential dread brought on by the pointlessness of it all.

People most likely to enjoy it: Children, anyone who hasn't played on a real golf course, those on psychedelic drugs.

Potential expansion: Following their unexpected success in 2008, the American team have proposed the Ryder Cup of Mini Golf. That way they can get to hoot 'n' holler and stomp all over the greens without it being considered "terribly bad form".

Expect to hear: "Aim left of the windmill and bounce it off the pig's nose and you've got a chance of making par."

Raised holes deter even the best putts.

History

In 120 years of production, the planet's motion picture industry has turned out in the region of four million features. Of these, around 15–20 per cent are considered sequels – they centre on returning characters, events or locations, or are part of a wider franchise that links separate works thematically. And of these 400,000 works, about six are considered worthy of the original works that inspired them. Hollywood was stunned when relative newcomer Francis Ford Coppola managed to turn Mario Puzo's mafia potboiler *The Godfather* into a major hit, but that was nothing compared to their bewilderment that he could outdo his work on the original by producing a sequel of such staggering quality in the imaginatively titled *Godfather: Part II*. Krzysztof Kieslowski's commission to produce a trilogy of works based both thematically and visually on the French *drapeau tricolore* could have been – should have been – an exercise in self congratulation of the most masturbatory kind, rather than the stunning collection of works that together formed the masterpiece he gave the world before moving onwards and upwards. And *Jackass Number Two* was pretty good. Especially the bit with the bees and the marbles. Sadly, for every *Three Colours* trilogy, there's a *Jaws* quadrilogy. For every *Godfather: Part II*, there's a *Godfather: Part III*. An original idea taken, twisted and turned into something no one who loved the original idea wishes had ever been brought into existence. All of which brings us to mini golf, the *Phantom Menace* of sporting pastimes.

You'll Need...

To be taking a holiday somewhere rubbish. This is generally the only excuse for thinking a frustrating round of this cretinous game might be enjoyable. Resorts lacking nice beaches, parks or amenable climates are to have a course nearby. So that should include most of the U.K.'s holiday destinations. Courses will be only too happy to provide you with a cheap ball, first manufactured in 1968, and cheaper club.

How You Do It

It's just like golf with all the fun taken out. So, no nice views, no carts, no thumping the ball with a huge club at the start of each hole and not really caring where it goes, and no finding yourself on a fairly flat and perfectly kept green. The only part of golf that mini golf captures is the bit where you put your ball somewhere that it's really awkward to play your next shot from. And even then in real golf if your obstacle is man made you usually get to move it somewhere better.

Advanced

Sadly there are enough enthusiasts of this pastime – known internationally as mini golf – for it to warrant an international federation (the WMF) and regular competitions with decent cash prizes. What's even more depressing is that if you were to wangle an entry for one of these contests you would get played off the course. Decent players of the game at this level will be looking for a hole in one every time, whether they're sending their ball up a chute, through a ravine or up one tentacle of a giant squid and down the other.

Why You Shouldn't Bother

Do you really want to be humiliated by a five-year-old or spend two hours trying to launch a ball into a hippo's mouth? Exactly.

The 18th: Not the trickiest of putts, but try finding a way into the clubhouse afterwards...

Mountain Climbing

Should you be considering this sport, a quick reminder: mountains are treacherous and remote places, noted for jagged rocky surfaces, exposure to the elements and their lack of quality coffee shops with sofas and free Wi-Fi.

Country of Origin: Switzerland

Possibility of death or serious injury: Not as high as you might expect. No, much higher than that.

Embarrassing clothing: Many climbers choose to wear a light helmet, though they may as well tie a stick of celery to their head for all the good it will do.

Greatest hazard: Avalanches, crevasses, and being eaten by mountain goats are all fearsome hazards, it's true, but it's tough to beat falling thousands of feet onto jagged rocks as a foolproof way of leaving the planet. It has a certain high impact style, too.

Watch out for: Small shrubs growing out of the rockface. These might provide vital support for a few seconds before you continue plunging to your death.

People most likely to enjoy it: Bungee jumpers who find the elastic band ruins the fun.

Potential expansion: Climbing walls are becoming increasingly popular in gyms around the world and offer a safe way to enjoy climbing. An even more enjoyable alternative can be found in the new sport of Struggling up the Stairs With a Cup of Cocoa and Getting into Bed.

Expect to hear: "Just over that next ridge and we're there…"

History

For as long as mountains have been around, man has admired them from a distance, featured them in paintings and made up stories about lost worlds filled with fantastic creatures that lay just the other side of them. Not surprisingly it was the Victorians who came up with the idea that climbing up the things would make for an ideal activity to tax the frame, expand the lungs and turn young men's impressionable minds from impure thoughts. And so, young and old alike were indoctrinated with the idea that putting life and limb at peril in pursuit of a nice view from the top constituted an acceptable leisure activity.

You'll Need…

A natural aversion to lie-ins. Most serious climbers employ an "Alpine Start" for their

Typical. She forgets the rope, but is she going back for it…?

109

It's hard to quantify the fun and sheer excitement of staring death in the face up a vertical cliff covered in seagull shite.

summit runs. Although this means you're less likely to encounter melting ice at the peak, and therefore more likely to survive until tea-time, it does mean you'll need to set your alarm for 1.30am. And whilst traditionally the mountain climber set out with enough equipment to invade a small country the sport has shifted its emphasis, with most climbers now adopting the "Alpine Style" of minimal kit, minimal rations for low impact climbing. Many new climbers who might applaud this environmentally sound approach change their tune upon discovering that this means they'll have to make space in their knapsacks to transport their own bodily waste off the mountain. They'll also have learnt their first important lesson about climbing – namely that anything that comes preceded by the word "Alpine" is usually bad news.

How You Do It

The urge to climb is one that most people are born with. Sadly the key technique of belaying is one that needs learning. Belaying is the means by which the person you're climbing with saves your sorry arse when you inevitably screw up. Rather worryingly for them you'll need to return the favour. The key to effective belaying is paying out or reigning in enough rope at any given point to maintain the right amount of slack for the climber. Communication is also vital. The key commands are "On Belay?" to check that your partner is ready for you to start climbing; "Off Belay!" to inform your partner you have reached a safe spot and

they can relax; "Up Belay!" if you require less slack; and "Up Yours!" when you've got sick of being shouted at. It is also the responsibility of the advance climber to notify the belayer quickly and clearly of any imminent danger to them, ie "Rock!" in the case of loose scree, or "Falling!" if the climber loses their footing. This allows the belayer an extra split second with which they can take evasive action. It is not the cue for them to give a witty response along the lines of "'n'roll, dude!"

Advanced

Free soloing is at the most extreme edge of the minimal impact approach, and requires you to take on these behemoths of nature armed with little more than a cup full of chalk dust. The chalk dust – powdered magnesium carbonate – is used by the climber to improve his grip in conditions where a single slip will mean game over. Despite its dangerous image, injuries are relatively rare in this branch of the sport. Fatalities, however, are commonplace.

Why You Shouldn't Bother

Ask a mountaineer, "Why did you climb it?" and the standard response has always been "Because it was there". The fatuous logic displayed by this response sadly reflects the symptoms of High Altitude Cerebral Edema – just one of the many forms of altitude sickness you can look forward to taking home with you as a souvenir should you be lucky enough to actually make it back from your expedition.

Olympic Torch Carrying

The progress of the Olympic flame around the globe is inspiring and deeply symbolic and we owe a debt of thanks to that nice Mr Hitler for introducing it. So, no surprise that the Chinese embraced it so wholeheartedly.

Country of Origin: Germany

Possibility of death or serious injury: Usually low, but not so during the 2008 journey of the Olympic torch when the mere mention of Tibet could cause injuries consistent with having your head kicked in by a Chinese thug.

Embarrassing clothing: Dodgy matching tracksuits as worn by every German couple in the 1990s.

Watch out for: Sudden squalls.

Prize/Rewards: Carrying the torch is considered an honour, reward enough in itself. So, in a word, no.

Expect to hear: "Has anyone got a light?"

History

Life in ancient Greece can't always have been a picnic, what with having to deal with gorgons, sword-wielding undead skeletons and plumbing that was only slightly more advanced than the kind of thing you'll find in modern Greece today. On top of everything else, your every move was being watched over by a big brother style audience of fickle and feckless gods who could give you the head of a bumble bee and the legs of an ostrich should they feel like it, just by pressing the interactive red button. So it was nice to know that there was at least one person up on Olympus that the human race could count on taking their side. Prometheus' theft of fire for mankind's use was a remarkable sacrifice, the ancient Greeks commemorated his heroic theft in the form of a flame that was kept alight throughout the length of their Olympic Games. The flame was reintroduced to the games in 1928 at Amsterdam as a symbol of the original spirit of the games. All of which has little to do with the completely twentieth-century idea of Olympic torch carrying, which was dreamt up as a way to promote Nazi ideology prior to the 1936 Olympics.

You'll Need...

A heavy duty sponsor. Or six. In 1936 the flame was lit by a torch bearing the logo of Krupp, the conglomerate that kept Germany in munitions, Messerschmitts and mess tins throughout two world wars. At the last Olympics it was Coca Cola, Samsung and a computer firm no one's ever heard of. You'll also need a few witless, photogenic celebrities to add some glamour to the proceedings and run in the right direction.

How You Do It

Olympic torch carrying has become a lot trickier since the world's population has woken up to the fact that it's increasingly used as a promotional gimmick for the host country and the commercial sponsors looking to maximise their profile. It's also managed to become a focal point for world protest – so much so that the Beijing organisers had to employ a crack team of security staff/Tiananmen Square veterans to intercept "torch botherers".

Why You Shouldn't Bother

Did I mention the Nazis came up with this...?

Orienteering

The sport of orienteering is an interesting blend of map-reading and cross-country running... and if you're very bad at it, a lost-in-the-woods Hollywood slasher movie.

Country of Origin: Norway

Possibility of death or serious injury: Anyone not wishing to find out just how serious extreme exposure can be is advised to stick to a pleasant ramble in clement weather.

Embarrassing clothing: The cagoule. Enough said.

Watch out for: Bogs, old mine shafts, Scooby Doo, precipices, the cold, the rain, snow, wild animals, barbed wire, and animal traps. And that's just on the way from the car park.

Expect to hear: "This pit I've fallen down wasn't marked on the map. And where did all these bones come from?"

History

Our planet's culture has rarely taken a major turn as a result of any influence from Scandinavia. Denmark gave Shakespeare a hero who died of indecision, Sweden's gift to the world was IKEA flatpack furniture and its accompanying impenetrable instructions, and Norway gave us the miasmic theatre of Henrik Ibsen. So it's of little surprise that competitive getting-lost-in-the-woods is Scandinavian.

You'll Need...

Orienteering courses aren't known for being littered with tourist-friendly route markers complete with "You Are Here" arrows. You'll get the map the second the race starts. You'll also be wanting a compass, preferably one that didn't come out of a Christmas cracker, cross-country running gear, a whistle, and a personal punch card. This is for collecting patterned punches from the control points you happen to stumble across in the course of the ramble through the woods you'll take while you wait for the emergency services to come and find you. Assuming the bears don't find you first.

How You Do It

The good news is that the start of the race is staggered, which is pretty apt since that's how you'll be crossing the finish line too, should you be lucky enough to make it that far. Staggered starts are fairly standard for orienteering events as they reduce the chances of you bumping into your competitors and asking for directions. This means that you can sprint off into the undergrowth at an impressive speed after only the most cursory of glances at your newly acquired topographical course maps. As soon as you can you'll be able to dive out of sight behind a bush and ask the three big questions: what is the compass direction and elevation of my first control point? Why didn't I pay more attention during the map-reading seminar the organisers put on? And most importantly, whose stupid idea was it to come on an orienteering course in the first place?

None of the man-traps will be marked.

Oxford vs Cambridge Boat Race

As well as being places where the children of the privileged go to learn to drink, have sex and take drugs, universities have also traditionally been associated with the pursuit of sporting excellence. Though not usually when it comes to rowing.

Country of Origin: England

Possibility of death or serious injury: Remote, provided you know how to swim.

Greatest hazard: Drunken chavs throwing bottles of WKD and Smirnoff Ice off Putney Bridge at you.

Watch out for: The odd log or submerged tree floating downstream, launched jointly by the rowing crews of Goldie and Isis (the reserve teams who never made it into the main boat).

Prize/Rewards: Rowing blues get to keep their oar, which will become a major interior design eyesore throughout their lives.

People most likely to enjoy it: The type of oily, mendacious, trough feeding, perverts who will later worm their way into high office.

Potential expansion: Oxford and Cambridge already have the varsity rugby match, so using this great book to expand their horizons we suggest varsity bog snorkelling, finger jousting and punkin' chunkin'. Which would prompt the conversation: "Are you a rowing blue?" "No, I'm a bog snorkelling blue."

Expect to hear: "What a lovely sight! The Oxford crew have thrown their cox into the river!"

History

The petty aquatic rivalries of two sets of chinless wonders from the U.K.'s two most self-congratulatory educational establishments have been covered in the wider media for the 154 years that they've been meeting on a stretch of the Thames to pit their wits and flex their pecs against each other, watched by crowds of half-cut onlookers who are all praying that at least one boat sinks.

You'll Need...

Three A* A-levels, at least. Both Oxford and Cambridge have worked hard in recent years to become more open with their admittance policy and accept students from wider and more diverse backgrounds. As a result of this broadened outlook you're now likely to find the sons of Indian electronics magnates and the daughters of Russian oligarchs rubbing shoulders with the dim-witted members of the British Royal family and establishment

Members of the League Against *Double Entendres* like to keep the cox and the stroke a long way apart.

heiresses who have traditionally made up the academic population of these elite institutions. You'll also need to be between 6'3" and 7'11" in height. Either that or 5' nothing and very gobby with it. In which case you can be a cox.

How You Do It

Despite its amateur status, training is taken very seriously and competition for places is intense, particularly since amongst the supposed eggheads it's not unknown for students to pop up whose only major qualifications are places waiting for them in their native country's Olympic team. While the majority of competitors do prove their academic worth, the alleged amateurism of the race is undermined by the success of many of its participants in later competitions. Since the four-mile race is conducted upstream and goes ahead regardless of weather conditions it's safe to say that the genteel image of the race masks the effort involved. The collapse from exhaustion of a Cambridge crew during the 2002 event indicates what's expected.

Advanced

Throughout the last two centuries, the universities of Oxford and Cambridge have provided Great Britain with many of their greatest and most gifted leaders. Gordon Brown went to Edinburgh. Tony Blair went to Brighton Poly and John Major did a correspondence course. Anyway, in keeping with these traditions politics has frequently played a big part in inter-team relations, both in terms of issues relating to team dynamics and training but also over wider issues relating to the wider student community. Oxford student rowers staged a mutiny in 1959 (about a tightening up of training restrictions), then again in 1987 (about the dropping of an American rower).

Why You Shouldn't Bother

Getting into Oxford or Cambridge is hard enough in the first place. Getting yourself rowing blue status is no pushover either. That's before you embark on a ten-month training programme of getting up at 5am every morning — a time that is frequently left off student clocks — with no guarantee you'll get selected. All that time would be far better spent getting drunk, chasing freshers, forming dodgy rock bands and doing all the other things our planet's leaders do in preparation for high office.

The Boat Race is a national institution. Everyone tunes in to see if their team sinks or not.

Paintballing

Just like fascination with female breasts and not being able to ask for directions, even when hopelessly lost, an infatuation with guns seems to be hard wired into the male psyche.

Country of Origin: USA

Possibility of death or serious injury: Serious injury is rare, but you are guaranteed to come away looking like you've been given a kicking by a swarm of gnomes.

Embarrassing clothing: Serious paintballers will have their own kit, up to and including specialist helmets and larger-than-average ammo belts, plus their own meticulously cleaned gun (and a detailed technical knowledge of every gun on the market and why theirs is a better choice). If that doesn't come under the heading "embarrassing" then what the hell does?

Greatest hazard: If you're a manager, expect every person you manage to gang up in order to deliver as much pain as possible without actually pistol-whipping you.

Watch out for: The paint grenade.

Prize/Rewards: The admiration of 11- and 12-year-old boys.

People most likely to enjoy it: Single males that own all three *Rambo* movies on DVD.

Expect to hear: "You gotta ask yourself, 'Do I feel lucky?' Well, do ya, punk?"

History

While gun culture has permeated all forms of the media ever since the things were invented, relatively few members of society have been given the opportunity to run free-firing them at will – notable exceptions being members of the armed forces, the LAPD, and introverted American teenagers. That all changed in the early 1980s when two friends decided to take a device used for marking trees or cattle and set to work devising an arena in which grown men could act out the schoolyard combat fantasies of their childhoods. Albeit with little paint-filled balls standing in for the imaginary bullets of their youth.

You'll Need...

A CO_2 powered gun and a pair of work goggles for entry-level paintballing. If you're just looking for a fun day out…well, you won't be going paintballing in the first place. But most venues will be happy to sell you extras at extortionate rates. Ventilation at the lower part of the mask ensures that you'll be able to breathe. It also means that while that area of your face is protected, if you get hit there you can still look forward to a mouthful of paint.

Not so much Dirty Harry.
More like Messy Marvin.

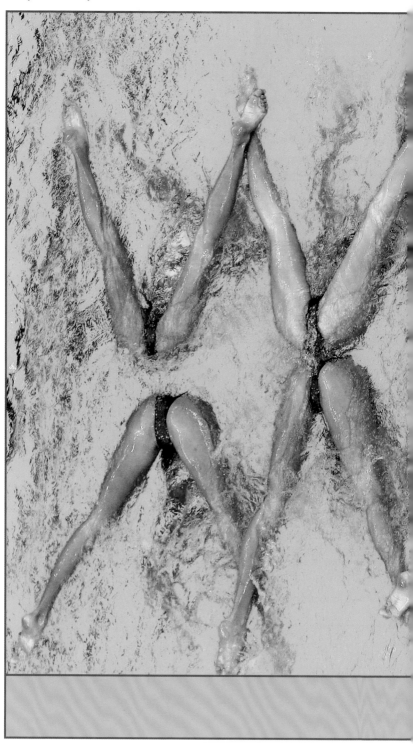

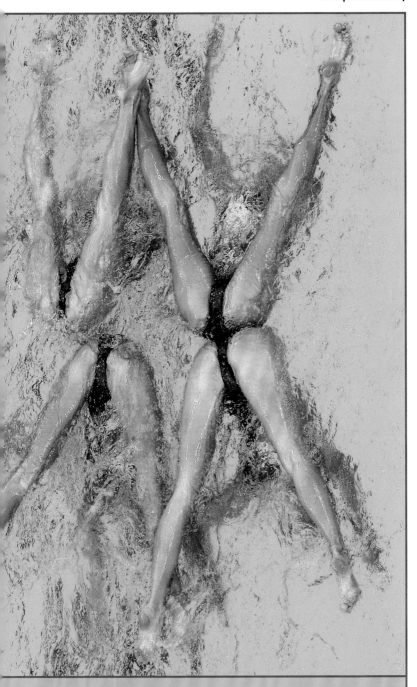

The Russian team's attempt to represent mitochondrial cell division through the medium of synchronised swimming was widely praised across the scientific community.

How You Do It

Whether your party opts to play "Catch the Flag", "King of the Hill" or "Find somewhere nice to sit away from all the psycho once-a-week paintballers", it's important to know that you can't aim for the head in most games. Which can make the game kind of tough since that's the place you would aim for first in actual combat and is frequently the only bit that's ever exposed. Blindfiring is also discouraged, and for wiping away paint once you've been shot you can get ejected. Making it an ideal way to bring your enforced paintballing career to an end if you're there for reasons beyond your control – an idiot friend's stag weekend or an enforced bonding weekend for work that leaves your team more splintered than ever, for example.

Advanced

Overshooting or bonus balling is frowned upon officially and is often punishable by a one-for-one elimination penalty. But in reality subjecting someone to a bit of pain is something you rarely get the chance to do in everyday life and is one of the few limited pleasures of the sport. This is particularly true

You were cleaning it? Yeah, right.

if you're on one of those stupid weekend bonding exercises and the target of your bonusballing is the idiot manager who proposed coming paintballing in the first place.

Why You Shouldn't Bother

If it's warm when you play you'll sweat. If it's cool you'll freeze. Either way you're guaranteed a rubbish time. Statistically it's safer than tennis. But the harm that it does to you won't be physical, it'll be social. "What are you doing this weekend?" "I'm going paintballing." "Oh, is that for someone's stag?" "No, I'm part of a league." Sound of tumbleweed blowing through the middle of the conversation.

Is it Jack Bauer, Dirty Harry or Rambo...? No, it's Martin from Data Entry.

Paper, Scissors, Stone

Considered by some as merely a pastime, bouts can last longer than fencing and be more confrontational than WWF.

Country of Origin: Japan
Possibility of death or serious injury: There's always a chance that a particularly pumped player is going to be over enthusiastic when blunting your scissors. It's a risk you gotta take.
Embarrassing clothing: Attracting, as it does, a scraping of freaks and weirdos there will be a full range of idiotic outfits and costumes at any event.
Watch out for: "Scissors...no, stone...no paper...doh!" and a mad glint in their eye. This may be their only opportunity in life to shine and God forbid you get in their way.
People most likely to enjoy it: Knuckle dragging competitors with a Mohican whose grasp of rules maxes out at two or more.
Expect to hear: "Dude, it's mano-a-mano."

You'll Need...

One hand for an amateur level bout, both for a pro game (see below). You'll also need attitude. Whilst organisers of professional contests have yet to turn this once innocent activity into an offshoot of Lucha Libre wrestling, they're certainly giving it their best shot, with larger than life contestants.

Advanced

Governing authorities such as the WRPS (you can guess what the initials stand for) insist that advanced players of the game hold up their choice behind their backs with their spare hand. This prevents players from gaining any advantage by making or changing their choice based on that of their opponent. Judges assigned to watch each player will inform the referee of any violation. It also shows that there truly is nothing on earth that America doesn't believe it can't work out with a suitably anal approach, a bit of legislation and a couple of impartial observers.

History

Paper, scissors, stone – or rock, paper, scissors, if you're American and therefore have a pathological tendency to mess with rules, spelling and anything else that doesn't quite conform to your view of the world – is a game which has been played by colleagues, siblings and couples throughout history as a way of determining who takes responsibility for something that both parties are keen to avoid doing, from taking out the trash to sleeping on the wet patch. Only in North America could it become a professional sport.

Two left hands are not compulsory.

Parents' Race

School days are supposed to be the happiest days of your life – but not if you live in fear of your overweight dad insisting on running the 100m on school sports day.

Country of Origin: Unknown

Possibility of death or serious injury: You may appear alive and well, but coming last will ensure that you remain dead to your offspring forever more.

Embarrassing clothing: Yes, if you bring running spikes or look remarkably well-kitted out to run 100m. You ruin the whole "it's just a fun event, no big deal" forced nonchalance.

Watch out for: There's always one parent who was a minor athletics prodigy in their youth and still trains regularly. Choose the lane next to them and trip them at the start.

Prize/Rewards: The brief flicker of something other than total shame at being associated with you in your child's eyes.

People most likely to enjoy it: The grown-up versions of the kids who liked beating you at athletics at school.

History

For one day of the year, the children of the world go to school with smiles on their faces and joy in their hearts. Textbooks and teaching are left aside as teachers and pupils alike celebrate life in a series of good natured contests in a spirit of seasonal cheer. Yes, the last day of term before the Xmas break is pretty much the best day of the year as far as just about every member of the school community is concerned. Sadly it's in stark contrast to that most loathed event of the school year, Sports Day. A day when ritual humiliation is virtually guaranteed for all but an unbearably smug few. The particular lowlight of this day of shame for all concerned comes in the shape of a seemingly impromptu but all too predictable call for those parents who've bothered to take the day off from their jobs to support their offspring and get in on the action.

You'll Need...

To look unprepared. When the announcement is made, pretend you haven't heard it. On no account be the first parent standing up. Once three or four others have made their way over to the starting line you can look around in surprise, laughing dismissively and mouthing non-aphorisms such as "What?" "You're kidding!" and "Oh, no!"

Why You Shouldn't Bother

You must come in the top three. Anywhere else and your child will be silently pitied by their classmates at best and violently bullied at worst. It can scar them for life and it's all your fault. Yes, it is.

Children whose parents work for American investment banks will enjoy the rich irony of competing in the sack race.

Parkour and Free Running

Both of these barmy urban cults espouse efficiency as being at the cornerstone of their cod philosophies. So why not accept this and be truly efficient by using the streets and their furniture for the purpose they were created for, namely walking along, sitting on or chucking rubbish into.

Country of Origin: France

Possibility of death or serious injury: More a probability than a possibility.

Embarrassing clothing: Absolutely not. There are stiff penalties including a lifetime ban for anyone wearing anything less than cutting-edge street fashion.

Greatest hazard: Certainly not misjudging a leap and falling 75 metres on to the pavement, oh no. Tripping and falling on your bum and thus looking uncool is considered by far the greatest danger. Zut alors!

Watch out for: Film crews making endless anti-perspirant adverts.

People most likely to enjoy it: The perpetually late for work.

Potential expansion: Efforts to expand free running and parkour into the countryside have proved futile. Somehow jumping over the occasional ditch doesn't seem to offer the same thrill and spectacle.

Expect to hear: "That lamppost wasn't there yesterday."

History

While free running and parkour claim to be vastly different activities, they share many key components and are categorised together here due to the striking similarities they share, and more importantly to cause maximum annoyance to members of both fraternities. While parkour is based around notions of purity, economy and efficiency, free runners are more concerned with expressiveness, acrobatics and earning huge wedges of cash by acting as consultants for rooftop chase sequences on Hollywood action movies. To the casual observer, however, there may be little to differentiate between the two forms, as in both cases practitioners seem merely to be jumping over stuff as if their life depended on it. Both schools can trace their ancestry back to the barmy pastime of point-to-point walking, a particularly Lutheran method of going for a stroll where the walker is encouraged to maintain a straight-line route regardless of whatever obstacles present themselves. Given that it's based on a refusal to shift from a course of action, regardless of what harm or damage comes of it, it's no surprise to learn that point-to-point walking was incredibly popular with U.S. President Theodore Roosevelt. But it was a Frenchman, Georges Hebert who came up with the idea of actually putting together a bunch of stuff specifically to make life difficult for anyone looking to get from A to B as quickly as possible, and his development of obstacle courses for the military gave the name to the modern movement.

You'll Need...

Cool clothes. For a sport that claims to have a spiritual basis, a lot of emphasis is put on the kind of superficial surface stuff you wouldn't have to worry about before a game of tennis or a quick swim. Most importantly clothing should not look new. It should be a little *fatigue*.

How You Do It

You jump around, over, under and through stuff – lampposts, walls, fences, cars, buildings. Both parkour and free running require excellent spatial awareness. So if you're the kind of person who normally bumps into stuff when you're walking down the street at normal pace then chances are neither of these is for you. Painful encounters with kerbs, walls and pavements are a key part of the experience for anyone learning the techniques, so you might want to start at home. While city streets are the traditional setting for this kind of activity, you'll find that carpeted surfaces and soft furnishings tend to be a bit more forgiving than the concrete, metal and broken glass you're likely to encounter in an urban environment. Most importantly, anyone wanting to be taken seriously in either the parkour or free running movement should never question the point of what they're doing. This is one sure-fire way to join both opposing communities in a rare moment of harmony as they unite in their contempt of a non-believer in their midst.

Advanced

Parkour disciples' biggest beef with free running right now is its growing commercialisation, with money flowing into the sport and the first World Free Running Championship staged back in September 2008. Advocates of free running have responded that the sport is simply evolving, and that, anyway, those parkour saddos are just jealous amateurs and as stuck in their ways as people who say that pro cycling should be drug free.

Why You Shouldn't Bother

Devotees of both cults need to realise that there is already a name for those unfortunates who spend an excessive amount of time utilising the facilities provided by an average city street. They're called the homeless.

Reclaiming the streets for acrobats and mime artists everywhere.

Polo

Tradition has it that the game was originally played with the head of an enemy rather than a ball, so avoid playing with elderly Iranians who like to play it old school.

Country of Origin: Iran

Possibility of death or serious injury: The bumps, bruises and broken limbs traditionally associated with falling off a horse and being hit with large mallets.

Embarrassing clothing: As with so many sports it's all about context. Loud shirts with tight jodhpurs and boots look fine on a polo ground, but crap in a city centre bar.

Prize/Rewards: If you can afford to play polo then you are already so rich that any prize will be utterly meaningless to you.

People most likely to enjoy it: If you appear on a rich list and Prince Charles and Prince Harry are your idea of good company then polo could be just the ticket.

Potential expansion: It's highly unlikely that the riff raff would be able to afford it.

Expect to hear: "Has Charles gorn and fallen orf again?"

---

affairs that entire villages get involved in, either as players or spectators, and where keeping score is less important than coming together as a community in a spirit of friendly competition. The British realised there was something more to be got from this game and did all they could over the course of the nineteenth century to iron out a few of the kinks that they perceived in the game – namely, the community element, the lax scorekeeping, and the lack of a decent pith helmet. But they did keep the horses. After all, there's nothing closer to the British royal family than their horses, which in some cases bear a strong familial resemblance.

One's captain attempts a short.

History

Polo is something that's existed in one form or another ever since man first noticed that the flat-backed animals running around with long faces seemed altogether to be very trusting and amenable creatures and decided to set about enslaving the entire species for his own use. Forms of the game were played, and sometimes still are, across Eastern Europe, Asia, South America and the Middle East, which involve anything up to 100 players a team. These tend to be chaotic and riotous

Fox Sports: Bringing you the top events from around the world. Tonight – rat basketball.

Just like Buzkhasi but with better uniforms, and this time the old goats get to watch.

You'll Need...

Three gifted horse-riding mates for the most widely played version of the sport. And ponies. Ponies for everyone. Not Shetlands either. Fresh ponies are needed after each chukka, of which there are always at least four and can be as many as eight. Oh, and they're not technically ponies either, they're proper horses, and generally thoroughbred at that, and almost all trained for a period of two years from the age of three in how to play the game. Anyone with any understanding of the cost of stable fees will appreciate that it's not called the sport of princes for nothing. Although given the decline in influence of monarchy it might be better renamed the sport of Russian oligarchs, software developers and Simon Cowell. You can imagine that he in particular would appreciate the high-waisted trousers worn by the players, and probably already has a pair like that at home. And ever since working with Paula Abdul he's developed an eye for what features to look for in a horse too.

How You Do It

Polo is unique amongst team sports in that amateurs – usually the team patrons – regularly hire and play alongside the sport's top professionals. Which when you think about it is a lot like having a situation in the playground where the kid whose ball it is gets first pick. Also second, third and fourth pick. That tells you pretty much everything you need to know about polo, other than the fact that this is another segregative sport where lefties are anything but welcome. Left-handed players, that is.

Advanced

If this all seems a bit unostentatious for you – perhaps you're one of the many foreign slaves labouring under the brutal yoke of the English Premier League, say? On a mere £120,000 a week. Anyone looking for a more exclusive version of the game will no doubt be delighted to hear it can also be played on elephants.

Potholing

Those with a generally nervous disposition or a specific phobia of bats, bugs, heights, enclosed spaces, deep water, the cold, the dark or the unknown might want to consider something a little less nerve shredding. Amateur bomb disposal for instance.

Country of Origin: USA

Possibility of death or serious injury: High. Both are possible and neither is likely to be improved with experience. Because the more experience you have, the deeper you like to go. And you'll be stuck in places where the only light source is a faintly luminescent mould... and the only chance of help is from a faintly luminescent mould.

Watch out for: Wobbly stalactites, impending flash floods, rock falls.

Prize/Rewards: Potholers dream of discovering unseen subterranean wonderlands, but almost always just find a lot of pitch-black, terrifying tunnels that a mole would have a squeeze getting into.

People most likely to enjoy it: If you like eating raw fish and asking people what they have in their "precious pocketses", you'll be a natural potholer.

Expect to hear: "I thought *you* were bringing the torch."

History

For as long as there have been stars in the sky and leaves on the trees, man has been getting lost, spraining his ankle and reduced to living on a diet of bugs and his own urine before dying a slow and lonely death down one of the ruddy great holes that permeate the planet. But it's only very recently that he's been doing it for fun. Potholing is a sport that anyone can participate in, if not actually enjoy, and since the deepest and most treacherous caves represent one of the few remaining unexplored regions of the planet, there is a great deal of scientific value attached to potholes, mostly concerning the warped psychology of why anyone would want to go down one of them as a leisure activity. Prolific amongst twentieth-century cavers was Clay Perry, an American outdoorsman who coined the term "spelunker" as a nickname for caving enthusiasts for reasons that no one has ever quite worked out. Though Perry proved himself a competent caver, having to be rescued from almost certain death no more than a dozen or so times in his caving career, his affectionate, if somewhat bizarre, term rapidly became associated with the amateurish, low-end and almost-certainly-bound-to-end-in-disaster breed of explorer who ventures forth on expeditions armed with little more than a Zippo lighter and a cheese sandwich.

You'll Need...

As many light sources as you can carry, a hard hat, and a capacity for distinguishing between one scary looking rock and another if you're

Ooh, that looks a lot of fun.

Most people's idea of hell. The potholer's idea of a great place for lunch.

planning on actually making it out again. Plus a long roll of string to show you where you've been.

How You Do It

It's generally agreed that a team of four is a good number of people to go potholing with, as if one person gets into trouble then two of the team can go for help (and assist each other on the way out) while one team member stays with the stricken individual. A team of four also means that no one is left on their own when the inevitable arguments start about whose turn it was to bring lunch, which passage to take, and why saving money on cheap unbranded batteries was not such a great idea after all. And what that terrifying noise was.

Advanced

Speleological societies have sprung up all over the place and as if you didn't have enough to worry about, they've made it very clear that there are specific do's and don'ts when it comes to descending into the bowels of the earth. And funnily enough the most important of these is to ensure that the outputs of your own bowels are not left to stink out the otherwise oh-so-fragrant underground caverns. Potholers should be aware that just because it

all looks pretty scary and hellish, the underground has its own very delicate ecosystem which should be respected.

Why You Shouldn't Bother

British horror movies haven't been up to much since hammy Hammer Horror days, but *The Descent* managed to capture the sheer terror you're likely to experience if you make the decision to go pot holing. Even before the monsters turned up.

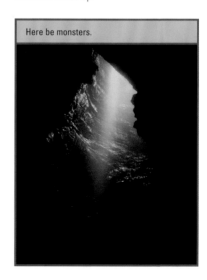

Here be monsters.

Pro Competitive Eating

Regardless of their nationality, for reasons of convenience most professional eaters choose to base themselves in the States, and no doubt feel suitably inspired by the highly gifted amateur community of walking water beds they find themselves surrounded by every day.

Country of Origin: USA

Possibility of death or serious injury: We all hope so.

Embarrassing clothing: It's worth remembering that no garment with an elasticated waistband has ever been seen on the cover of *Vogue*.

Greatest hazard: Remember Mr Creosote in Monty Python's *The Meaning of Life*? That could be you.

Watch out for: Hurricane-like flatulence. When you're responsible for a national weather alert, you know you've gone too far.

Prize/Rewards: Competitors will find there is such a thing as a free lunch, provided you like 112 hard-boiled eggs for lunch.

Potential expansion: Yes. Lots of potential for expansion.

How You Do It

Techniques will vary depending on the event. The first is the slow-but-steady approach. The second is to stuff your mouth as full as you can and keep it stuffed at all times, relying more on the combination of saliva and peristalsis to do the work for you than actually chewing. This is a lot more gross and therefore makes for better television.

Why You Shouldn't Bother

Competitive eating is probably the only sport in the world where the governing body actively discourages any form of training. That training has in the past usually involved stretching the stomach lining with excessive water intake. Since this can lead to seizures and brain swelling and can in exceptional cases prove fatal, pro eating can clearly be as dangerous short term as it is long term. It's worth noting that despite its image, many of the world's top pro eaters are actually remarkably svelte. Japanese pint-sized pro eater and pop star Natsuko Sone is a mere 43kg in weight.

History

Often referred to as "gurgitators", competitive eaters first came to prominence at the dawn of the twentieth century at county fair sideshows. Nathan's Hot Dog Eating Contest is one of the longest running prize competitions and has been running at Coney Island on July 4th since 1916. The Independence Day slot seems entirely appropriate since these contests are celebrations of the right of every citizen to stuff their faces.

No dispute as to who ate all the pies.

Professional Wrestling

Pro wrestling may not be the only sport on the planet where the outcome is as sewn up as an election in Zimbabwe, but it is possibly the only one you can't put a bet on.

Country of Origin: Mexico

Possibility of death or serious injury: There are plenty of casualties. Common causes are steroid abuse, accidents during carefully choreographed wrestling bouts and blow outs in overdeveloped egos.

Embarrassing clothing: You'll be wanting something that says "superhero", albeit a scantily clad superhero. What you'll get is "tosser in spangly knickers".

Greatest hazard: Being upstaged by a wrestler called "The Nippletwistillator".

Prize/Rewards: You'll get great big piles of cash, kids will buy dolls of you, and you may even get the chance to show off your lack of acting skills in a Hollywood movie.

People most likely to enjoy it: Anyone who has huge hair, a larger-than-life personality and likes slamming their oiled body against another chap's while wearing studded leather pants.

Expect to hear: "After you with the baby oil."

---

of D. H. Lawrence's *Women in Love* when Oliver Reed and Alan Bates got their kit off and wrestled naked in front of the fire. Many are trying to. But the most remarkable event in the history of professional wrestling is one that's occurred relatively recently – namely its controversial decision to cease being a sport at all and simply become an adjunct of the entertainment industry. While no one seems quite sure when this happened, the split between the North East U.S. Promoters and the National Wrestling Alliance – and the subsequent formation of the World Wide Wrestling Federation in 1963 – is generally acknowledged as the point at which pro wrestling stopped being about actual sporting competition and simply became an absurd collection of preening retards strutting about in a garish pantomime of simulated violence and breathtaking narcissism. And while this bizarre form of performance art quickly lost favour even with its more intellectually challenged audiences across Europe, it has become a huge hit in the U.S. and with a worldwide audience of windowlickers lured in by overpriced and idiotically named events such as WWE Wrestliania and WWW Bitchslap – The Reckoning. Or maybe even Super Seize-Up Slamdunk Sunday.

History

The sport of wrestling has a rich and noble heritage that's featured in everything from the plays of William Shakespeare to the video games of the Nintendo Entertainment System. Who can forget the scene in Ken Russell's film

You'll Need...

An image. Comprising an outlandish costume, a catchy name, a signature move or eight, a silicone-enhanced partner, and a history that incorporates some bad blood back down the line with an already established wrestler.

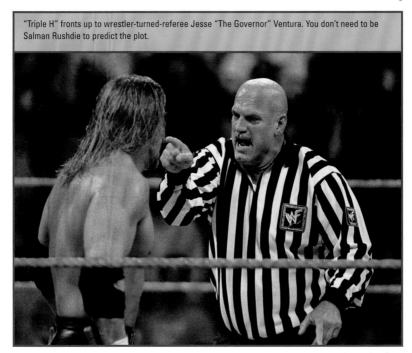

"Triple H" fronts up to wrestler-turned-referee Jesse "The Governor" Ventura. You don't need to be Salman Rushdie to predict the plot.

How You Do It

While college students pursuing the sport at amateur level will spend hours working on core strength and balance techniques in order to give themselves an edge in the ring, such work is pointless at pro level. Still, the good news is that you don't have to worry about winning or losing. All that will have been sorted out well in advance of the actual bout. Which isn't to say that you won't need to put the training hours in. As well as maintaining a physique that doesn't have the pay-per-view audience reaching for the remote you'll need to learn more set moves than an NFL quarterback and learn not to take it too personally when things go a bit wrong and you unexpectedly get a misplaced fist in the groin or your opponent realises the chair he's just smashed over your head wasn't one of the balsa wood breakaway props after all.

Advanced

With plotlines that make the history of the Borgias resemble an episode of *The Tweenies*, the best way to ensure a higher profile within the world of pro wrestling is to create the kind of scandal that the reality TV-fed sub-literate audience will lap up. Blackmail, adultery, and sibling rivalry all go down well, and the biggest names in the business have often re-launched their image by switching from being a face – the "heroes" of the ring – to being a "heel", or villain in the pro wrestling world. All of this goes down very well with the huge worldwide audience and also helps distract everyone else from the real life doping and accidental death scandals that have plagued the sport for the last ten years.

Why You Shouldn't Bother

Pro wrestling is essentially a very bad TV reality show but with jockstraps and elbow padding. Anyone with a desire to take part in either would do well to get professional help. What is even worse is the confusion that has been caused between the WWWF World Wide Wrestling Federation and the WWF World Wildlife Fund whose logo incorporates a lovely, cuddly panda and whose patron is Prince Phillip – The Greek Destroyer.

Punkin' Chunkin'

Pumpkin hurling isn't confined to the hour after sampling a new Jamie Oliver recipe. No, in the U.S. people are as serious about hurling pumpkins as they are about the right to arm bears.

Country of Origin: USA

Possibility of death or serious injury: Only if you look down the barrel of a loaded pumpkin hurler.

Greatest hazard: High velocity orange gourds are considered a menace to afternoon strollers and air traffic.

Watch out for: Little old ladies with four white mice and a sparkly stick.

Prize/Rewards: Your massive investment in time and money will earn you a couple of inches in the local newspaper and all the mashed pumpkin you can throw away.

People most likely to enjoy it: Those who think that *Scrapheap Challenge* is a bit too wide-ranging and needs focus.

History

There is one sport where the machine is everything. Where the abilities of rival competitors are restricted almost entirely to their input at the design phase. A sport that was born in Delaware, and has never left home. A sport that begs the question, "Why does it only happen in Delaware?" And the answer is...because it's called punkin' chunkin'.

You'll Need...

A catapult, slingshot, pneumatic air cannon, trebuchet (or other device as sanctioned by the sport's authorities) that is capable of hurling a full-size pumpkin the best part of a mile.

How You Do It

Decide which class you're in. There are 12 in total, ranging from "Adult Centrifugal Human Powered" to "Youth Air". Note that the category "Youth 10 and Under" refers to the age of the entrant, rather than the age of the machine. Though once you see the work that goes into building these contraptions you'll quickly realise that it'll take you around a decade of weekends to knock something together that meets competition standards.

Advanced

For an attempt to count, all pumpkins must leave their launchers still in one piece. To ensure this is the case, many competitors have taken to developing their own new varieties. So that'll sew up your spare time in the evenings for the next ten years.

Why You Shouldn't Bother

See below. You get to meet people like that.

The authorities fear that there might also be a punkin' chunkin' dance.

Rally Driving

The World Rally Championship is less about driving on difficult terrain around the world and more about picking up an interesting variety of exotic roadkill. As one famous rally navigator once said: "Left over crest, into short 4 right, opens 60 left...SHEEP!"

Country of Origin: France

Possibility of death or serious injury: Yes, and rally drivers like to spread it around the audience, too.

Embarrassing clothing: A big helmet that will really accentuate the fact that your head is bobbing around like a cat in a tumble dryer. Rally fans still represent the largest percentage of bobble hat wearers left on the planet.

Watch out for: Hedgehogs, rabbits, dogs, foxes, badgers, goats, pigs, sheep, cows, deer, boar, kangaroos, but never possums. Though one legendary Kiwi driver was actually nicknamed Possum Bourne.

People most likely to enjoy it: If your pride and joy is a souped-up Ford Ka with smoked glass windows, alloy wheels and *Knight Rider* light effects on the front grill, then you probably should be on *Pimp My Ride* and not into rally at all.

Expect to hear: "I said left! What? Well, that was the next left!"

History

In the early days of the twentieth century, the similarity of vehicles meant that there was little difference between a Grand Prix car and a "rally" car. It was only when the race cars started losing the on-board mechanic and were streamlined into single-seaters that there was a noticeable difference. That and the fact that rally cars went up scary mountains while Grand Prix cars stuck to the flat. Rallying really took off in 1911 with the inauguration of the Monte Carlo Rally. France was the hub of world motorsport having hosted the first Grand Prix in 1906 and the first 24-hour race at Le Mans. This achievement is still celebrated each weekday evening by French drivers circulating around the Arc de Triomphe in Paris trying to take each others' door handles off.

You'll Need...

One of the central appeals of rally driving for its fans is that most racers use production line models, or close relatives of them, so finding a vehicle to compete in shouldn't be too much of a challenge. What might prove a little tougher to come across is a very patient, very understanding mate to act as your navigator. While rally drivers get to floor it on roads where the speed limit's been suspended, skid round corners spraying gravel over spectators and generally see the world doing something

Ruining a perfectly good cactus photo.

they love, their navigators spend the whole day hunched over the map on their lap barking orders that are ignored or at best poorly executed, but which in any case are taken without so much as a "thank you". The navigator then can look forward to a night planning the next day's route and compiling pace notes while their drivers are getting pissed up with a bevy of fawning rally groupies, should such a thing exist.

How You Do It

As a sport, rally driving comes pretty close to real life, albeit on a fairly extreme day. The only time you get to drive slowly you're normally going sideways. Its competitors get to drive on public roads, in the kind of cars driven by the general public, at speeds which would normally mean losing your licence. The view you get is like a police chase video except faster and with no transit van in front of you dropping stolen goods out of the window. And the spectating public get to be so up close and personal that they can literally smell the action. All good fun, but in an increasingly litigious society the sport's governing bodies have had to introduce measures that generally discourage the killing and maiming of said public, unless absolutely unavoidable. Which it wasn't for many years. The Mille Miglia, one of Italy's premier events,

came to an abrupt end in 1957 when a tyre blow out led to the death not only of driver Alfonso de Portago but also that of his navigator. And eleven spectators.

Advanced

One of the forms of the sport that's grown in popularity in recent years is historic rallying. These nostalgic events feature entrants competing in lovingly restored antique vehicles. The emphasis is less competitive, with entrants happy just to get to their final destination in journey times that the modern driver would be appalled by. So all in all it's a lot like taking a trip on one of the U.K.'s modern commuter trains, only more fun and less expensive.

Why You Shouldn't Bother

Rally driving may be a little on the dangerous side, but you do at least get a seatbelt and a helmet. That may be of little comfort on the precipitous climbs through Corsica and Crete where the only barriers on the bends are a couple of small rocks and a breeze block or two. Another downside is that you would be getting into a sport Mark Thatcher was famously involved in, but at least you know he's already got the title of "worst rally driver ever" sewn up.

That's got to be 150 points at least...

Real Tennis

Amongst its many other claims to fame, real tennis is proud to boast some of sport's most eccentric terminology. For instance, specialised serves include the "railroad", the "bobble" and the "poop".

Country of Origin: France, naturellement

Possibility of death or serious injury: With the possibility of death so high in everyday life, the medievals didn't really go in for extreme sports.

Embarrassing clothing: For total authenticity players should wear hose, long pointy shoes, a codpiece, and smell of sweat and dirt.

Watch out for: A skillfully executed poop coming at you.

People most likely to enjoy it: Prince Edward is a great fan. That says it all.

Potential expansion: No. Contraction.

Expect to hear: "Hah, I'm going to serve a giraffe."

History

Real tennis is the distant, hideously deformed cousin of lawn tennis that should be confined to the soundproofed attic of history for its own safety and the safety of others, were it not for a small collection of idiots determined to see it parade itself in public. Its regal roots gave it the name royal tennis, an alias it still goes by in Australia. Real tennis can safely beat lawn tennis in court exclusivity. With a mere 35 courts available for use worldwide you're guaranteed to get into the Top 200 rankings. If they had them.

You'll Need...

With courts in such limited supply your best bet for a game, should you be demented enough to want to play, is to commandeer the enclosed stable yard of your parents' country estate.

How You Do It

The major differences between real tennis and lawn tennis are as follows: the ball can bounce twice at the service end, initiating a "chase"; the ball is only served from one end, the other end being referred to as the "hazard" end; serves must touch the "penthouse" above and to the left of the server; a "hazard chase" may be called when the ball bounces twice at the receiving end, but only on the half of the hazard end nearest the net. It's no surprise to learn that the game's most famous player was King Henry VIII, who clearly amended the rules of the game to suit his own purposes in much the same way as he played fast and loose with the laws and religion in order to divorce and/or murder his wives. The enclosed area makes playing shots off the surrounding walls and ledges the key to success. For instance knocking the ball through a "window" is a good way to advance the game and win points. On your average housing estate it's probably a sure-fire way to start a knife fight.

Why You Shouldn't Bother

Life is too short for an incomprehensible game played on a court you can't find.

Keeping it real. Keeping it real complicated.

Relay (4 x 100m)

At its very heart, relay is a sport about ascribing blame for failure. Since there will always be a weak link, and since it will always be 100 per cent apparent just who that weak link is, what's to be gained by joining a relay team?

Country of Origin: Sweden

Possibility of death or serious injury: After an especially poor performance a team member may need to have a baton surgically removed.

Embarrassing clothing: Modern male runners such as Linford Christie have pioneered running shorts in which it is possible to see genitals bobbing about like a fourteen-year-old boy's head at a Metallica concert.

Greatest hazard: A slippery baton.

People most likely to enjoy it: Ghoulish spectators hoping that they get the kind of baton carnage evident in the historic Beijing 100m relays where a team of marathon runners were able to claim the bronze medal in the final simply by not cocking up their handovers.

Expect to hear: "Don't snatch!"

History

The relay was devised to get a few more people in on the act of running round the track rather than standing at the side watching. Envious of swimmers who get to perform at 50, 100, 200 and 400m distances in freestyle, breaststroke, backstroke and butterfly (and while we're on it, what in God's holy name is the purpose of butterfly? When have you ever been at the pool and witnessed someone butterfly past you?). Thus the relay was born. Which the swimmers also nicked. The traditional relay team comprises four runners, one of whom is very fast and three of whom are not as fast. This means that relay is by its very nature a sport steeped in so much rivalry, jealousy and resentment that if it had been around in Chekhov's day he would never have got around to writing *The Cherry Orchard*. Instead he'd have written a five-act play about four athletes in their twilight years who've never got over placing second in the Moscow Games of 1900 because one of them dropped the baton.

You'll Need...

Three mates, preferably ones you don't like all that much as chances are you'll soon be despising them. Also a baton.

How You Do It

The generally accepted strategy is to start with the second fastest runner, then the third fastest, then the slowest and finish with the fastest. You can expect your first round of heated discussions in determining who goes where. Next you'll need to come up with an agreed method of handing over the baton, at which point the toys should really start coming out of the pram. Finally, round off your training session by agreeing on whether your handoffs will be blind or sighted. If you're still speaking to each other by the end of your first training session you'll be doing better than most.

Advanced

The 4 x 100m relay event is traditionally the final event in any athletics meet, meaning that there's bound to be an enthusiastic and appreciative crowd to witness your histrionics when the wheels finally come off your misguided attempt to present a united front to the world. It's a no-win situation for the best teams because if you have the fastest runners you're expected to win.

Why You Shouldn't Bother

If you're the fastest runner in your team then it will be your job to be eternally disappointed and quietly nurture resentments for your team-mates and their sub-standard efforts in practice and competition. If you're the slowest runner in your team you'll have a life experience similar to the fat kid in *Lord of the Flies* – occasional outbreaks of outright hostility surrounded by long periods of patronising civility that barely hides the seething frustration felt by your colleagues for your evident lack of worthiness. There may be some comfort to be had by the two team members in the middle positions of this hellish little ménage a quartet, but one can only suspect they live in fear of their own promotion to the role of denied champion or worse still, demotion to the role of village idiot. All of this would be – if not irrelevant – largely qualified, if you could be guaranteed to win every race. Which, of course, you won't – making relay a team sport that can only truly be enjoyed by the psychologically sado-masochistic.

A beautifully executed 4 x 100m relay is like watching a well-oiled locomotive go up through the gears. But most spectators want to see the train crash.

Rodeo

Should you be unlucky enough to find yourself in a rodeo, hold tight and bear in mind that however much you may hate the experience of sitting on top of a raging bull, you'd hate being underneath his stamping bulk even more.

Country of Origin: USA

Possibility of death or serious injury: Whether you're being trampled by a horse or tossed off by a bull, it's guaranteed to be a little ouchy.

Embarrassing clothing: Generations of cowboy movies and the Village People have ensured that leather chaps, waistcoats and ten-gallon hats never truly go out of style.

Watch out for: Some of the most terrified clowns on Earth.

Prize/Rewards: Massive cash prizes and a hill o' beans.

People most likely to enjoy it: Yee-hahs and yippe-ki-yays.

Potential expansion: Mechanical bulls are increasingly popular, and offer a way to find out if you have an aptitude in comparative safety. They are particularly popular among women, especially those for whom the washing machine has recently lost its magic.

Expect to hear: "Do I have to ride that one? He looks kinda angry…"

History

Generally speaking, sports don't tend to be based around the experience of the working man. The International Olympics Committee has yet to recognise, for example, the potential for events such as synchronised shelf stacking or freestyle plumbing. But the sport of rodeo is one which has its roots firmly planted in the world of the weekly grind, albeit as practised by one of history's most glamorous occupations – the cowboy. In spite of everything Hollywood has told us, the life of the cowboy was not one filled with squaring up to guys in black, fending off tomahawk attacks on speeding stagecoaches and farting round campfires. Rather it was a world where the working cowboy was required to herd, brand and capture for slaughter his stock in the shortest possible time. And given that said stock quickly learnt what getting trussed up meant for them personally, this proved something of a challenge. After a long tradition of inter-ranch contests designed to test these skills, the first major rodeo competition was organised by Buffalo Bill in 1892. Since then rodeo has continued to reflect the importance of the working man realising his dream in the good old U.S. of A.

You'll Need…

The range of events available to a novice rodeo rider are as many and varied as the injuries they're likely to pick up, and the kit you'll need

Woooahh! No one saw *that* coming.

A great night for Hank who takes his personal best up to 3.756 seconds.

will vary accordingly. The roughstock events – bareback riding, saddle bronc riding and bull riding – are generally considered the most dangerous and as a result you'll want to ensure you protect those bits of yourself you'd rather not have either a bronc or a bull riding roughshod over. A cricket box or a pair of socks will do the trick and should also nicely fill out your distressed Levis. Timed events such as steer wrestling, team roping, tie-down roping and barrel racing require greater mobility of their competitors and so you will probably wish to forgo the pant padding and possibly even trade in your Cuban heels for a good pair of trainers. Most importantly, don't forget to chew on some beef jerky so that at the end of the event you can spit a celebratory/disconsolate bolt of manly looking cowboy saliva in a convincing manner.

How You Do It

Bull riding is one of the oldest events in the rodeo, and remains one of the most popular for audiences. The simple reason for this is that it affords them the greatest chance of seeing someone get hurt. While man has a history of forming productive working relationships with members of the animal kingdom, there's no evidence to suggest that a bull has ever felt like doing anything for a man other than gore him and stamp on his head. Should you be unlucky enough to find yourself in this event, hold tight and bear in mind that however much you may hate the experience of sitting on top of a raging bull, you'd hate being underneath one even more. Make it to eight seconds and you'll have earned a qualified score.

Advanced

The closest the U.K. gets to rodeo is watching wilfull sheepdogs ignore their owners' whistles and shouts. But the 1924 London International Rodeo at Wembley Stadium is acknowledged as the most successful rodeo in history. So any English visitors to rodeos in the USA might like to inform their stateside cousins that we had one of them in London. But it was much bigger.

Why You Shouldn't Bother

A survey of 28 sanctioned rodeos in 1994 found that the injury rate to animals based on more than 33,000 completed runs was 0.00047 per cent. So if anyone is getting hurt it'll be you.

Roller Derby

With female boxing, Thai boxing and nude mud wrestling all growing in popularity there's little doubt that there's an audience for female contact sports. Why make the women involved wear short skirts, fishnets and fight on roller skates? Well, why the hell not?

Country of Origin: USA

Possibility of death or serious injury: Yes, but there are worse ways to go than being mown down by a herd of high school girls on roller skates. The DVD will certainly be memorable. You might even make YouTube "video of the day" alongside a croissant that looks like the Virgin Mary and four college students setting light to something.

Embarrassing clothing: Some militant feminists might find the outfits demeaning, but then again some might say that compared to beach volleyball or nipple tassel netball they are overdressed.

Greatest hazard: Breaking a nail... in someone's eye socket.

Potential expansion: Roller derby refuses to die so there's obviously a market for young girls getting physical with each other. Who would have thought it?

Expect to hear: "Eat elbow, bitch!"

History

The 1930s Depression was a depressing time for everyone. Out of desperation promoters hit upon the idea of marathon events – walkathons, danceathons, and almost inevitably skateathons. Leo A. Seltzer's 1935 roller marathon was entered by 25 teams competing on an oval racetrack in a bid to cover the distance between San Diego and New York City. During the race – which lasted the best part of a month – there were inevitable collisions, crashes and open aggression between competitors who were effectively competing for the right to eat...and so a sport was born. Doing away with the vast distance that was needed to be covered and allowing for a greater degree of contact between opposing players gave the sport an opportunity for the violence that quickly became its hallmark and also meant that audiences didn't need to sleep in their seats while they waited for the result. Roller derby's revival in the 1970s made the sport a largely all-female affair, and whilst male audiences took delight in watching girls in shorts and knee pads get nasty with each other, many social analysts hailed it as an example of greater equality and means of social expression for the female gender. They're pedalling the same line for its current revival too, which just goes to show how far sociological analysis has moved on since the 1970s.

You'll Need...

Heavy mascara, big hips, sharp elbows, an Amy Winehouse attitude to life (but maybe not her training regime), long legs and breasts. Roller skates and pads are a good idea too, though of secondary importance if you don't fulfil the first specification.

How You Do It

Play starts serenely with both teams setting off anti-clockwise around the track. Penalties are given to skaters who trip, punch, fight or behave in an unsporting manner. These players are also awarded sponsorships, endorsements and bonuses by venue operators who know all too well what the crowd have paid their hard earned cash to see.

Advanced

As with so many sports, the devil is in the detail when it comes to what's allowed and what isn't. Elbows are allowed to be used to block for instance, but that does not give licence for players to redesign each other's noses with them. Not when they've paid good money for a cute little Britney Spears push button. Of course when you're speeding around a banked track on rollerskates hoping your make-up doesn't get too mussed up before that cute guy arrives, it's sometimes hard to tell when an assertive block becomes something a little too aggressive even for roller derby's fluid set of absurd rules. In any case, all it usually takes for the fight to start is one dodgy call by the hapless referee, so you can be certain that trouble is never that far away.

Why You Shouldn't Bother

The current revival that roller derby is enjoying has largely had to happen without the assistance of specialist banked tracks (the shortage of midget velodromes continues). Still, as the sport grows and attracts a new generation of young, sinuous, female competitors, so roller derby's natural audience of middle-aged men in raincoats will no doubt return. Perhaps the popularity of the sport is emblematic of the tough economic times we live in, ie the nearest thing we've had to a Wall Street crash since the Wall Street Crash.

Being a wide-ass prima donna is no drawback in roller derby. Great news for J-Lo's career planner.

Rugby

Rugby is named after Rugby School where William Webb Ellis first picked up the ball and ran with it. If he'd been attending Our Lady Immaculate school, it might have been a lot more cumbersome.

Country of Origin: Not Wales, actually.

Possibility of death or serious injury: Both, though only the most extreme cases of death will stop players joining the after-game beer fest.

Embarrassing clothing: Rugby players enter into the fray dressed as insulated from danger as your average ping-pong player. And they're proud of it.

Greatest hazard: Being passed the ball. In most amateur games of rugby the wingers are the safest on the pitch as it never gets out to them.

Watch out for: Anyone on a stretcher. They are considered out of play and should no longer be hurled to the ground and given a hiding. Unless you can make it look like an accident.

Prize/Rewards: You could become a national hero and your dentist's best friend.

People most likely to enjoy it: Those who enjoy spending Saturday afternoon with their head wedged up someone else's bottom.

Potential expansion: Rugby is already played worldwide, often by people who couldn't be bothered to read the rules properly.

Expect to hear: "Oh, was that your *head...?*"

Scrums are thinly disguised excuses for homoerotic contact.

having thighs you'd struggle to get both arms around – rugby has formed the template for many a nation's variation on a classic territorial game played with an odd-shaped ball. The Americans have taken rugby, added a couple of C-130 transporter planes worth of equipment and bent the rules to allow forward passes to create American football. Meanwhile, in Australia they've cut the sleeves off their shirts, increased the size of the pitch and added an extra goalpost.

You'll Need...

Fourteen mates if you're playing rugby union, 12 mates if you're playing rugby league, and someone who cares enough to know the difference. Plus someone to explain the rugby union scrummaging laws – as what you *can* and *can't* do changes every year and it's only the professional referees who can be bothered to read the whole rulebook. You'll also need a prolate spheroid ball, which sounds like the kind of injury you're likely to get playing it. You'll also need studded boots for ensuring you get maximum traction as you step into your opposite number's face during the ruck. And not forgetting the phone number of a good physio,

History

Cited as a hooligan's game played by gentleman – the gentlemen in question weighing an average of about 18 stone and

a competent osteopath and some kind of injury counselling service in case the scars run really deep.

How You Do It

The object of rugby is to gain territorial advantage whilst in possession of the ball to allow your team to place it in your opponent's end – score a try – or kick it through their goal to score points. In recent years both forms of rugby have seen their rules shift, and these changes, whilst causing a certain amount of debate, have allowed the game to take a high profile place on the world stage and attract a truly international audience. The people least affected by the fluid nature of the rules have been the players, whose key objective remains to kick, maul and stamp the living crap out of each other. But not get caught doing so.

Advanced

One of the key indicators that proves rugby to be little more than an excuse for 30 men to engage in violent behaviour is the almost complete absence of safety equipment. Some players will sport a gum shield, not so much to protect the jaw as to look like Jaws from the Bond movies of the 70s. The front row wears overtight and rather grubby looking Alice bands that no one can quite fathom the point of. And given the size of your average prop no one is about to argue about it. Players are allowed to use bandages to prevent excessive blood loss during a game (i.e. any more than three pints, four if you're playing for Wales). Perhaps it is the near certainty of casualties that makes everyone so incredibly polite about the physical atrocities being perpetrated. "Sorry, was that your face? I do apologise." Even the ref gets treated with decency and deference. Unlike football, where the ref gets yelled at for 90 minutes and the players fall over clutching their face and then holding their head like they were in an amateur production of *Titus Andronicus* if someone so much as brushes past them.

Why You Shouldn't Bother

Rugby is a game for gentlemen hooligans. Unless you are one, best to avoid. There are easier ways to find beer buddies.

Australia on the attack. That'll be a try, then.

Running of the Bulls

Despite its reputation, this is not just an activity for the young and reckless. The last runner to be killed was a 63-year-old veteran, proving that age doesn't necessarily guarantee wisdom.

Country of Origin: Spain

Possibility of death or serious injury: Yes – anything from a sprained ankle to complete death. Fifteen people have been killed, the last in 1995. There is also a much higher percentage of gorings compared to most athletics meetings.

Embarrassing clothing: Yes – the little red scarf and white shirt make all the runners look like air stewards on the campest low-cost airline in Europe. Accessorize with a cute little red sash.

Greatest hazard: Look behind you! Animal rights activists sometimes pledge to "go naked" as a protest against the sport's cruelty to bulls. When it comes down to it most turn up in swimwear. Some hardcore protest, eh, strolling round Spain in a bikini.

Is it expensive? Not really, but you probably won't wear your running gear much after you're finished with it.

Watch out for: Drunken backpackers who've stayed up all night and are not sure which direction is downhill.

Prize/Rewards: A sense of achievement that you have cheated death and two angry horns.

People most likely to enjoy it: Ernest Hemingway, when he wasn't so large. Or drunk. Or dead.

Potential expansion: The Bull Ring shopping centre in Birmingham.

Expect to hear: "El toro! Vamos!"

History

For a nation whose national sport is ganging up on farmyard animals, running in front of a load of charging bulls comes naturally to them. The bull run takes place every day of the week in the northern Spanish town of Pamplona as part of the festival of San Fermín. It used to be a rite of passage for every young virile Spanish male, but in the last 50 years a large proportion of the runners taking to the streets have been tourists.

For some inexplicable reason, the pre-bull-run protests are beginning to attract as big a crowd as the event itself.

Bulls rarely fall for the, "I'm jus' sleeping off a heavy night" routine.

You'll Need…

The good news is that bull running – or *el encierro* – is far more accessible for Joe Public than bull fighting. You won't need six poncily dressed mates idiotic enough to join you, you don't need to have studied for ten years at matador academy, and you're even allowed to be upset at the sight of blood, since any that gets spilt is likely to be yours and therefore worth getting upset about.

How You Do It

Whilst bull running is a strictly amateur entry event, there are a number of professionals involved. While the entrants run ahead of the bulls, you'll find a team of trained herders running behind them. With thinking like that, it's not hard to see how they got to be pros. Plus they get paid to be there. The runners gather in Cuesta de Santo Domingo, where they sing an ode to a statue of San Fermín :

A San Fermín pedimos, por ser nuestro patrón, nos guíe en el encierro, dándonos su bendición.

Though it's tempting to give the translation as: "Dear San Firmin. What the ***** have I let myself in for" it actually means: "We ask San Fermín, as our Patron, to guide us through the Bull Run, giving us his blessing." Ernest Hemingway would have done just that when he took part.

Advanced

Not surprisingly, injuries are common. Unlike bullfighting it's not just the bulls on the receiving end of it either. The cobbles of a narrow Spanish street tend to be a bit slippy underhoof. So if this isn't a cross-species marketing opportunity for Nike I don't know what is. "Just Gore it!"

Why You Shouldn't Bother

Bulls are majestic and proud creatures. But like a generation of modern man, their inability to bear children or produce milk has left them feeling a bit surplus to requirements. While modern man has beer, internet pornography and the words of Jeremy Clarkson to help him feel a bit better about himself, the male cow has little but the prospect of a quick death. The last thing it needs is some smart-arse tormenting from a nation that gave us the word *machismo* but who lost the 1898 war with America in about half an hour.

Runners can buy a picture taken from 'Bull's Arse Cam' after the event.

Shuffleboard

Shuffleboard has proved so popular amongst senior members of the community because it involves even less physical activity than bowls, which has all that nasty bending and leaning involved.

Country of Origin: Dreamt up in International Waters

Possibility of death or serious injury: Only if the ship sinks.

Embarrassing clothing: An octogenarian's notion of what constitutes jaunty sea-going attire: sandals, socks, peaked caps and of course leather chaps.

Prize/Rewards: It's not the winning, it's the taking part that counts. Because by the time you've got back to your cabin, you'll have forgotten who *did* win.

Expect to hear: "Since the operation, the shuffleboard is the only thing I have to get up for in the morning."

History

Apart from "walking the plank" and "Roger the cabin boy", the nautical world has given us few games to play. Shuffleboard, though, is one of them, being a sport that is played almost solely by the wandering denizens of the ocean – cruise liner passengers.

You'll Need...

An ocean-going vessel with a deck size capacious enough to account for a standard shuffleboard court, which is 39 feet long and six feet wide. Shuffleboard courts are always defined in imperial terms and don't appreciate being referred to in modern metric measurements, so they're probably illegal in the European Union. The court is marked out in scoring zones from 1 to 10, but it's quite hard to see which is which. They used to make them a lot clearer you know.

How You Do It

Shuffleboard is best played in teams, as the more players you have involved, the greater the chance of someone remembering the rules. Put simply, shuffleboard is like curling without the ice or the constant sweeping up.

Why You Shouldn't Bother

If you're on a cruise ship and this is the most interesting thing they've devised for your amusement, then you should be after a refund.

It's a great way to meet some honeys.

Ski Jump

With a current world record of 239m for a super-grande-deluxe-class jump, some clean underwear is probably a good idea.

Country of Origin: Norway

Possibility of death or serious injury: High, so it's deeply frustrating that Eddie Edwards suffered neither.

Embarrassing clothing: The kind of ultra-tight unitard that is usually reserved for experimental dance groups and mime artists.

Greatest hazard: A small mistake when landing can have disastrous consequences, so you certainly don't want both your skis dropping off in mid-air.

Watch out for: Boeing 747s in your flight path.

Prize/Rewards: Medals and a curious mixture of awe and incredulity from people you meet.

People most likely to enjoy it: If you're the kind of person who likes saying "wheeee"…

Expect to hear: "Eagles don't wear skis."

History

The sport of ski jumping will be celebrating its 150th birthday in 2010, when it will once again take pride of place in viewers' minds as the Winter Olympics event that is most instantly eye-catching but ultimately rather dull to watch for more than a minute or so. After a lengthy paternity dispute the father of the sport was revealed to be Norway's Sondre Norheim, whose initial record of 30 metres over a rock stood for more than 30 years, largely because none of his fellow countrymen were stupid enough to attempt replicating his stunt.

However, an outbreak of mass lunacy in 1862 led to the first ever national competition, which not surprisingly Norway dominated. Other countries soon got in on the act, wholly inappropriately in many cases. English sporting failure may well be something that's taken for granted these days, but it's safe to say that in the sport of ski jump a single Englishman was able to re-write the rulebook. Literally. By putting on a display of such ineptitude at the 1988 Winter Olympics, Eddie "the Eagle" Edwards stunned the Olympic committee who were hastily forced to redraft the criteria for qualification in order to prevent him from ever competing again.

You'll Need…

Skis. No poles are required, because frankly there's no point carrying something you'll only go impaling yourself on. With a current world record of 239m for a super-grande-deluxe-class jump, some spare clean underwear is probably a good idea. Finally, you'll need to get yourself to one of the stadiums where the biggest jumps take place. It's fair to say the best of these are all in Europe. The big venue is Holmenkollen, Norway, but there are good jumps throughout

Like ice speedway, ski jump is not generally covered under winter sports insurance policies.

He needs more cow bell.

adding the distance score to the three middle style scores from the judges. Then adding your age and subtracting the number you first thought of.

Advanced

At the moment there's a bit of a row going on about women's ski jump. This is strange given that the scoring seems to have been devised by the female mind, it not being all about size but also technique. The central issue is that there aren't many female athletes, so the sport's governing body doesn't want to start giving out medals as it feels the quality of competition will be diluted. However, in Canada it's against federal law to spend money on projects which discriminate. This has led to suggestions that more should be done to make the sport appealing to women whilst making the sport less interesting for the male population. The best suggestion so far has been to make Sarah Jessica Parker the sport's new figurehead.

Scandinavia, and it's taking off all across Europe. It is now proving as popular with the Austrian people as converting the cellar to give your family a bit more room.

How You Do It

Maintaining good line and body position on the run are key if you are to make it as far as the "K line" for the particular jump. Get to this and you have effectively made par, and get 60 points, with 1.8 points added/subtracted depending on how much further/how short you come up. The five judges also can award up to 20 points for style — body position, holding skis steady and wearing an outfit that complements the skier's natural colouring. Final score is determined by

Why You Shouldn't Bother

Unless you were born in a place with snow on the ground most of the year, you'll be rubbish at ski jump. And someone's already been famous for being rubbish at it.

Homenkollen. The theatre of dreams. The smorgasbord of despair.

Snail Racing

Several schools of thought exist as to the best way to race snails, none of which are of any interest to persons with an IQ above 20.

Country of Origin: France
Possibility of death or serious injury: Extremely low. Unusually for any event in which animals are involved, even the runners have a high survival rate.
Greatest hazard: French gourmands taking a fancy to your prized athlete.
Watch out for: Snail suffragettes.
Prize/Rewards: As with most "novelty" sports, participants are usually motivated by a misjudged desire to create an illusion that they are interesting people.
People most likely to enjoy it: Three-toed sloths. To them it happens all too quickly.
Expect to hear: "Ready, Steady, Slow!"

History

Snail racing is considered to be a French invention that was shrugged off by our too-cool-for-school Gallic cousins and embraced across the Channel. While the French will eat frogs, snails, dogs and horses, the English prefer to race them. Except the frogs.

You'll Need…

A snail that likes to get about a bit. Preferably one with a lightweight racing shell. Snail selection is important in this game and those that don't make the grade can easily be lobbed over the next-door neighbour's fence.

How You Do It

Snail racetracks are usually circular affairs a couple of feet in diameter with the starting

Randy male snails race towards a curvy little cutey with pheromones to die for.

Competitors must be able to sprint flat out on a variety of surfaces.

point at the centre of the circle, giving the overall impression that the entrants are racing to get off a dartboard. And let's face it, adding a few darts into the equation would probably add a bit of much-needed drama into the proceedings, albeit at the expense of a visit from the RSPCA. Trainers are encouraged to paint numbers on the shells, with a few bearing the colours of the sport's leading sponsors, the Royal Mail. Snails are encouraged to sprint off by a number of different incentives. These can include a bright green kos lettuce placed at the side of the snail arena, a horny female snail at one end of a track – dressed to kill – or they can be driven into a panic by the smell of crushed garlic cloves and the sound of a sizzling frying pan on the stove.

Advanced

With vast swathes of overgrown countryside, the English county of Norfolk has rapidly become known as the premier spot for the sourcing, rearing and training of world class snails, and not surprisingly the World Championships are to be found there in the sleepy village of Congham. Whilst some residents of the area feel that this gives their home a somewhat negative association, with a laughably pointless minority sport, most inhabitants admit that snails and coastal erosion are pretty much the only things to recommend Norfolk to tourists, there being a conspicuous absence of anything else of interest.

Training can be tough – especially the two-metre mud trail.

Why You Shouldn't Bother

Snail racing is the kind of mind-numbing, time-wasting and soul-sapping activity you can only imagine being enjoyed by those serving lengthy prison sentences. Or by those who engage in futile short-term bets.

Snooker

Snooker involves competitors nudging balls with a stick during hours of silence, so perhaps it's the feverish excitement and sheer drama of the game that attracts so many colourful, flamboyant characters.

Country of Origin: India. By the British.

Possibility of death or serious injury: Very low during the actual game though many players turn to drink and drugs in order to fill the aching void that awaits them all when their game starts to fail.

Embarrassing clothing: Snooker players are among the best dressed sportsmen in the world. It's only when you see inside their homes that they've furnished themselves (i.e. not got an interior designer to do it) that you realise they have about as much taste as an Inuit penguin chef.

Prize/Rewards: The kind of fake marble-pillared trophies – with a snooker player on the top – that only look good when placed in a skip or in a landfill site.

People most likely to enjoy it: The insane fathers of those players who have been remorselessly brainwashed into practising for 18 hours a day ever since they were old enough to hold a cue.

Expect to hear: "Oh, that's a lovely screw."

History

Never happier than when they were making simple things complicated, officers in the British Army in the days of empire took the game of billiards, added some extra balls in a melange of colours, drew up a bunch of insanely involved new rules and started insisting on penguin outfits for all players. And made the tables bigger. Although that may have happened later. In any case, the game of snooker was born. And for the best part of a century it's a sport that Brits have dominated, although now the top players are facing competition from players from the Far East such as Fu and Ding and many others whose names are shortened to make them read like a sound effect.

You'll Need...

The good news for anyone with an interest in the sport, if you're in a country where it's popular, is that snooker tables are very easy to come across, lurking as they do in low-rent halls on the cheaper side of town as well as in the clubhouses and country homes of the well-to-do. The bad news for rich man and poor man alike is that an interest in the game spawned by years of watching it on TV won't alter the fact that you will be utterly rubbish at it. Unlike pool, where vast numbers of options and the size of the table conspire to help even the rankest amateur pot the correct ball occasionally, snooker is actually reliant on a degree of skill that comes only with regular practise, something that most amateurs and even a champion player like Ronnie O'Sullivan seem rarely to be all that bothered with. Most halls will rent tables by the hour, at which point they'll unceremoniously turn the lights above your table off, plunging you and your party into monolithic darkness. You may be depressed by the fact that during this hour you've been unable to sink a ball, but rest assured, by continuing to play on in the dark you stand an equal chance of doing so.

How You Do It

Start by chalking your cue and looking moodily at the arrangement of balls on the table as if you are planning a shot, despite the fact that:

a) you have no idea what shot would be appropriate at this point; b) you wouldn't have the ability to pull it off even if you did know. Walking around the table whilst continuing to chalk up your already calcium overloaded cue tip can add to this somewhat pathetic charade. Now rest the thin end of your cue across the back of your hand whilst taking aim. Cue through smoothly, taking care not to snatch at the shot. Assuming you haven't torn a huge slice out of the baize, in which case any pretence of competence will already be out the window, step back and narrow your eyes as if guiding the ball into a pocket with the dark side of the force. Then shake your head regretfully and step graciously away from the table to allow your opponent to continue his demolition of you. Success at an early level is just hitting the ball you were aiming at (the cue ball doesn't count) and then doing it from increasing distance. Where the cue ball goes afterwards is totally irrelevant as "building a break" is still about two years away.

Advanced

Like many games which owe their origin to the English, the basic rules of snooker are supplemented by an elaborate and largely unspoken system of manners and etiquette. New players are reminded to take great interest in the play of their opponent and in particular to tap the base of their cue on the floor for each of the succession of decent shots played by their opponent, and to shake him warmly by the hand after he has completed his total humiliation of you.

Why You Shouldn't Bother

It's no coincidence that many of the world's top players have the kind of complexion you'd generally associate with the undead. Until someone invents a beach variation on the game this is a sport you'll need to sacrifice your daylight hours and a fair chunk of the night just to get barely competent at. Yes, they really do make it look easy on telly.

Removing the triangle before breaking off will help split up the reds.

Snowboarding

The animosity between the skiing and snowboarding community has already led to untold pain and anguish. It has promoted unrest, divided families and splintered the alpine fashion community.

Country of Origin: USA

Possibility of death or serious injury: There's a 60 per cent chance that you'll suffer one or the other within 30 seconds of leaving the ski hire shop. Injury can come via a number of interesting routes: snowboard/tree interfaces, big air tricks that go wrong, and – for those who can afford a helicopter to take them off-pisting – death by avalanche.

Embarrassing clothing: Off the slope, snowboarders are the kind of people who wear their trousers at mid-thigh level revealing as much of their underwear as possible. On the slope they'll dress exactly the same. But with a silly hat. Last season's O'Neill jacket is way too uncool to be seen in and the Oakley sunglasses have to be this year's.

Watch out for: Pile-ups at the top of the chairlift. Pisteurs and telesiege people generally hate snowboarders who struggle to get on chairs and drags and carve out their carefully-pisted ramps.

Prize/Rewards: A breathtaking panoramic view of the mountains as you are winched into the rescue helicopter.

People most likely to enjoy it: Surly teenagers who wouldn't be seen dead skiing with the parents who actually paid for their winter holiday.

Potential expansion: No, the snowboard and skateboard have fully saturated the idiot yoof market.

Expect to hear: "Man, I just caught some big air."

Go on, touch your board, that'll really help your landing.

History

First came the ski, then came the mono ski, then the snowboard and then the big fight.

Let's hope there's enough snow in the landing area...

You'll Need...

A board, boots, bindings and, above all else, a complete lack of ability. Whilst skiing places an emphasis on control, economy of motion and technical excellence, snowboarding's makeshift, make-do attitude prizes the sheer taking part above all else. This makes snowboarding an excellent sport for the athletically challenged, as a large proportion of the boarding community seem to spend about 90 per cent of their slope time lounging around in packs while they catch their breath, surreptitiously skin up and bang on about pulling a fakie without knowing what it actually means.

How You Do It

The basic starting technique for novice snowboarders is known as the "falling leaf". This is similar to learning to traverse on skis, but since the board remains pretty much perpendicular to the direction of travel it has the added advantage of creating the greatest possible surface area for anyone with a degree of competence behind you who might like to get past sometime that lunar cycle. Once you've got the hang of this you can move onto the more advanced form of falling leaf, where you'll still have your board facing at 90 degrees to the direction of the slope, but you'll be going down backwards. This greatly increases your chances of taking out one of those smug three-year-old skiers who is already showing more of an aptitude for getting down the slope than you, though less of a talent for causing total carnage on the way.

Advanced

One innovation that has caught the public imagination is boarder cross, a form of racing where instead of trying to beat the clock, competitors race the same course at the same time. This makes for an exciting sport that almost always involves at least one boarder getting wiped out, which might explain its popularity even amongst the skiing community, but should give you another good reason not to get involved without fully comprehensive medical insurance.

Why You Shouldn't Bother

Like so many things done well by experts, snowboarding looks fantastically cool. However, done badly by anyone over 25, it is like a desperate attempt to be down there with the kids.

The jump's kinda okay, but hey, those trousers are perfect.

Soccer

"The beautiful game" has swept the world, much to the chagrin of most Americans, who can't last 45 minutes without an advertising break.

Country of Origin: United Kingdom

Possibility of death or serious injury: Rarely death, but serious injuries happen in every Premiership game... until the player realises he's not going to get a free kick and stands up again.

Embarrassing clothing: Worse. Clubs are always changing shirts to maximise revenue and at £50 for a nasty nylon top it's the closest thing to daylight robbery there is. Apart from being mugged, obviously. As for barkingly stupid haircuts, football players have always been at the cutting edge of the ridiculous.

Watch out for: English players. The number playing in the English Premiership can be counted on the fingers of two hands. The same goes for the number of people attending Aussie football league games, where the players are given a programme of where all the spectators are going to be standing.

Prize/Rewards: Top soccer players earn a fortune, which will be spent on tasteless houses, orange women, and vast amounts of alcohol as their career declines.

People most likely to enjoy it: Those who think they're much better players than they actually are. They think they're Ronaldo but have the ability of Ronald McDonald.

Potential expansion: There's a big push to raise the popularity of soccer in the U.S. to European levels, though some body armour may have to be developed for the American game.

History

No one knows who invented football, or soccer or footie or "the beautiful game", which some marketing executive was probably paid $1m to come up with. The English introduced the rules, which were compiled by the newly formed Football Association in 1863, several members of whom still serve on the panel today judging by their general level of competence in managing the sport.

You'll Need...

Very little. The big attraction of the sport at grass roots level is intrinsically connected to the ease with which a game of football is set up, requiring little more than a ball, some players and jumpers for goalposts. With the international nature of top football, if you want to play at the highest level you'll need an extensive vocabulary of profanities – in as many languages as your underdeveloped brain can handle. You'll also need the kind of contempt for the refereeing staff that any normal person would reserve for a cold-calling insurance salesman ringing back for the third Sunday in a row.

Calling yourself a "soccer mom" seems to be a badge of pride in the States. "My daughter's on defense."

A classic pub game. One fit player waits for the other 20 to lumber up the pitch.

How You Do It

In keeping with the sport's humble origins, the rules of football are simple enough for anyone to understand. The aim is to get the ball in the opponent's net without using your hands – hence football. Unless you're a goalkeeper. In which case, you'll have a whole bunch of rules that seem to be designed to give you an unfair advantage over everyone else on the field. Goalkeepers are the mummy's boys of football and referees tend to give them an easy time, especially when the nasty, big, rough forwards invade their personal space. Not surprisingly, they're the only ones who are allowed to wear long trousers. If they weren't they'd only get their mums to write a note.

Advanced

Played by all ages and by both sexes, and watched by more people worldwide than have TVs, football has brought down more barriers, ended more wars and taught more English speaking peoples the importance of the silent z rule when pronouncing a name than any other sport on the planet. Naturally this situation has been far too good to last for very long, and as with all things where there is a buck to be made there's an institution to be ruined. Money has transformed the domestic game in the U.K. and as it sweeps the world many will ask questions about where it will all end, with good reason. Presiding over this fiasco is FIFA, whose decision to amend the offside rule has resulted in a situation wherein no one playing or officiating the game can explain the rationale behind any decision because the rule is of such complexity that it would give Stephen Hawking a migraine.

Why You Shouldn't Bother

As minor league clubs become about as economically viable as a chain of Cherie Blair charm schools, a kick around in the park is your best bet for a game of football. Or join a pub team where the level of activity trails off dramatically as fitness issues kick in after six to eight minutes. But whatever you do, don't expect a beautiful game.

Clearly not a Hereford United free kick.

Solo Yachting

Of the many people who have attempted this brave feat, a few have survived, and some have even managed to complete a circumnavigation. Which means that everyone is completely bored of seagoing nutjobs and after three months of nearly dying you won't even get your photo in the paper.

Country of Origin: Spain

Possibility of death or serious injury: Like many a Mafia boss before, you could be sleeping with the fishes.

Embarrassing clothing: You can wear what you like as long as you have something decent to wear going out of port, coming into port and on the video phone link.

Greatest hazard: The Bermuda Triangle, the Arctic Circle, Cape Horn, the Roaring Forties, the Doldrums, Billy Zane pretending that his shipmates have been killed by pirates, pirates – ahar me bucko! No, not that kind of pirate, Somalian pirates armed with AK47s.

Watch out for: The usual stuff: rocks, sandbanks, gales, icebergs, albatross, coral reefs, seagulls crapping all over the foredeck, sleep-deprived hallucinations, sea monsters and an owl and a pussycat in an attractive pea-green vessel.

People most likely to enjoy it: Ellen MacArthur, the hapless Tony Bullimore.

Expect to hear: "Alllll byyyyy myyyy-seeeelllllf, don't wanna beee…."

History

As centuries in history go, the sixteenth has to stand out as one of the most momentous in the development of the modern world. Ferdinand Magellan proved beyond any doubt that not only was the earth spherical, it was one of many bodies orbiting the sun in a universe that mankind, despite reaching the edges of his own explorable world, was only now taking even the smallest of first steps towards understanding. Sadly, Magellan went the way of many a maritime adventurer and perished at the hands of barbarians who saw European sailors as just another interesting meat to throw on the barbecue. It was only in the 60s and 70s when Frankie Chichester, Eric Tabarly, Robin Knox-Johnston and Chay Blyth started to blaze the trail that it really took off in a big way. Knox-Johnston's boat *Suhaili* was an inspiration to everyone that followed as it was the kind of vessel you'd hire to cruise round the Norfolk Broads in a gentle breeze, not something you'd think to throw at the Southern Ocean.

You'll Need…

A boat, an almost pathological desire to be all alone all of the time, and your holiday allowance for the next three years. Or six years if you live in the USA, two years if you live in France and the rest of your life if you live in China.

How You Do It

Attempting to complete a perfectly circular route around the planet would make this sport even more impractical and impossible than it is already, so the agreed course has simply to be one of at least 21,600 nautical miles, which crosses the equator, as well as every meridian in the same direction, and finish in the same port it starts, usually Southampton or Cherbourg. Both are towns with a rich naval tradition, and after having spent one night there, the prospect of spending 80 nights alone at sea doesn't seem too much of a privation.

French skipper Philippe Jeantot arrives in Australia during a 1987 round-the-world solo race. Sydney is one of only three ports to employ trained marsupials as pilots.

Advanced

Modern technology has made communication so much easier for the loveless solo yachter. GPS has allowed for more accurate calculations to be made during navigation. Red Bull means you've got a better chance of not dying in your sleep, though it does of course increase the chance that you'll be going to meet your maker with a funny acidic taste in your mouth. Finally, advances in satellite communication technology mean that there's virtually nowhere on the planet where you won't be able to call Samaritans from to cry down the line about how empty and meaningless your existence is. Assuming they haven't already blocked your number.

Why You Shouldn't Bother

Unless you're willing to risk life, limb and mental health in pursuit of a sport which will occupy your every waking moment – oh, and all the others too – avoid this sport as you would a date with Pol Pot.

This is the view for about 22,000 miles.

Speed Skating

Speed skating is all about precision, technique and a love of fabrics so tight that the world will be able to see what you had for breakfast.

Country of Origin: Norway

Possibility of death or serious injury: Fall over and it will feel like being mown down by a herd of cut-throat razors travelling at speed.

Embarrassing clothing: Oh yes. Think gimp suit but think high-tech gimp suit. Or an outfit from a Woody Allen sex comedy.

Greatest hazard: Being mistaken for a Mighty Morphing Power Ranger.

Potential expansion: None. Speed skating is in the top ten least compelling sports of all time and the only people who watch it are other speed skaters, for five seconds before wandering off to pick their nose.

Expect to hear: "I do not look like a human condom."

History

Take one standard size 400m athletics track, cover it with frozen water and voila – you've just ruined the finals of the women's 1,500m. But you've also created an approved speed skating track. Speed skating first came to prominence as a recognised sport in Norway, with competitions from 1863 regularly playing host to five-digit crowds, presumably members of the speed skating community who'd lost their other digits when they'd thrown down their hands in an attempt to break their fall, only to have them sliced off by the skates of other racers. Not long after that the Dutch rather cheekily organised an event which played host to competitors from exactly the same countries as the Norwegian competition, but which bore the lofty claim of being the

World Championship. While the events were sometimes invented seemingly on the fly, and the courses makeshift, the biggest issue at this point was timing, which on the whole was dodgier than a former royal butler who waits until he's sold a few million books to admit that he might have made most of it up. And that maybe it wasn't a "rock" that his former employer used to refer to him as but something that sounds similar. And starts with a "c". Anyway, controversy over race times aside, speed skating events grew in popularity with little changing until 1960 when racers competed on man-made ice for the first time. The funny outfits came later.

You'll Need...

Two major developments in equipment came into play during the 1990s. Firstly, the development of a new generation of hinged skates designed to remain in contact with the ice for longer as they are not affixed to the whole boot. These skates are known as clap skates. The ironic second major development, given that the skate used by professionals had now been named after an STI, was that all competitors had to compete wearing giant prophylactic devices. The World Health

Skaters must adopt a cartoon pose to start.

Organisation has dismissed the notion that they are somehow behind this blatant piece of subliminal sexual health education.

How You Do It

With the average speed for a men's race now at well above 30mph, the key lesson you'll need to learn is not "how to skate" but "how to fall on ice after you've been racing at a speed that you'd be unlikely to reach in a car anywhere in central Sydney." Sadly there seems to be no approved technique for doing this, so you're just going to have to get hurt.

Advanced

While the "freeze over an athletics track" approach has given Winter Olympics competitors suitable venues in the past, newer stadiums have been able to up the ante in terms of what's possible. For instance, the long track Olympic oval in Calgary has space for two ice hockey pitches at its centre — giving the audience something to watch while they are forced to endure the tedious periods in speed skating events.

Why You Shouldn't Bother

Speed skating's intrinsic problem is that nobody ever looks as though they're trying very hard. Even when they are. You'll look, and feel stupid. And unless you were born in a country that has 16 hours of night during its winter months and snowploughs parked on every street, chances are you'll be rubbish at it.

Competitors can also use their outfits at a variety of Amsterdam bars and nightclubs.

Speedway

To create speedway take any other activity involving motorbikes and increase the danger factor to the power of x, where x equals screaming "aaaaaaaargh" while every bone in your body is shaken.

Country of Origin: Australia

Possibility of death or serious injury: Riders are injured all the time in conventional speedway, but with ice speedway the tyres are equipped with spikes to dig into the ice. That's where it can get really *Texas Chainsaw Massacre*.

Greatest hazard: Falling off a motorbike at speed and then being run over by another motorbike. And then another, and another and so on and so forth. Slamming into the barriers when your throttle jams wide open or some joker takes your back wheel away.

Watch out for: Gravel in every part of your body.

Prize/Rewards: An ability to be the fastest motorcycle courier in the world when it rains.

Expect to hear: "Eat my dirt!"

History

While progress is generally seen as a positive thing, it is undeniable that there are certain things that are great fun to do but which it's nowadays frowned upon to enjoy. Smoking in restaurants between courses, hunting whales and powersliding a motorbike around on turf, throwing up grass, dirt and earthworms with no thought of the eco consequences. All of these things were done without a second thought or trace of apology in the 1920s and some more recently than that, in Japan at least. They were certainly happening in Australia before December 1923, when the first recorded speedway event took place at a showground in

Lower Hunter Valley, New South Wales. The open style adopted by riders soon proved popular for spectators in the U.S. and U.K., and despite a typically OCD British attempt to both tidy things up a bit and get in on shaping the rules by having the racers travel clockwise rather than anti-clockwise, the sport stayed true to its Aussie roots and soon swept the continent, presumably leaving a broad trail of mud, topsoil and massacred animal life behind it.

Today it's still popular across Europe and to a lesser extent North America. And while Australia was once the source of the world's greatest racers, they've been overtaken by Poland, whose riders not only do a better job quicker and for less money, they also arrive for race meets at the time they agreed with you on the phone. And don't just stand around all day drinking tea. And asking you if you've got any biscuits to go with that.

...and after the race he'll be happy to change your cistern.

Moto GP has the glamour, MotoCross has the drama and Speedway has gravel.

You'll Need...

A bike. One that runs off methanol, has but a single gear. Oh and no brakes. Did I mention that you might want to wear a helmet? And some padding. A lot of padding.

How You Do It

It's all about the powersliding. That means you'll be using the rear wheel to scrub off speed around the corners while still providing enough forward drive to get you round the bend. The bend in this case essentially being the entire length of the track, repeated four times. Needless to say, getting in front early is fairly important as the lead changes about as frequently as Bill Gates' sense of fashion.

Advanced

Recent developments have included the use of inflated fences in the British and the Polish Grand Prix. Not only have these significantly reduced the number of casualties involved in the sport since their introduction, they've actually increased the level of enjoyment for riders who've found that diving off their bike and bouncing off one of the barriers is a lot more fun than the race they're involved in. At the other end of the fun factor there's also a variation on traditional speedway – speedway raced on ice. With bikes fitted with spiked wheels to ensure maximum purchase in the ice, or soft sweet flesh of any fallen rider who happens to get in their way.

Why You Shouldn't Bother

Say what you like about sports involving motorcycles – they are all inherently cool. What's more they'll help you develop the skills that might give you a chance of beating the odds and not becoming just another of the casualty statistics in which motorbike riders feature so prominently. That is unless the motor sport you develop a fondness for is Speedway, where the chief skill is to ride a bike with both wheels facing virtually any other direction than the one you're travelling in – and which is competed on low-riding bikes that wouldn't hold out for five minutes against the onslaught of speedbumps.

Squash

Squash is a game played in a court resembling the solitary confinement cell in a high-class psychiatric prison by two people who spend the whole time doing their best to get in each other's way.

Country of Origin: United Kingdom

Possibility of death or serious injury: Low, unless someone locks you in the court over a weekend. A few people have got eye injuries from a high-velocity ball and ear injuries from a friendly whack on the head. But, as they say, if you can't stand the heat, what were you doing playing squash in the kitchen in the first place?

Embarrassing clothing: Squash goggles make you look like you should appear on the latest *Crimewatch* poster.

People most likely to enjoy it: Agoraphobics.

Expect to hear: "You so did get in my way."

History

Developed at Harrow School, squash's unique selling point, if you can call it such a thing, is that it's played with a broken ball. Whilst in other sports a ball will be discarded once it goes flat, this is the only kind of ball available to those playing squash.

You'll Need...

Squash is possibly the only sport in the world where it's not just the players that warm up beforehand. Squash balls are very much the Mariah Careys of the sports supply store, demanding, as they do, a warm-up of their own before they'll take part in your game. The question, 'Why not just play with a ball that isn't jiggered in the first place?' is a fair one that has yet to be satisfactorily answered by the sport's governing body. Anyway, the trainer manufacturers would also have you believe that you'll need another pair of shoes to clutter up the dustball collection under your bed. Tennis shoes don't give the right grip for the court's smooth indoor surface and cross trainers are not cut out for the high-impact nature of the game. However, think about all the things in the world you need more than a pair of special shoes just for squash.

How You Do It

You hit the ball against the wall. Your opponent does the same. Repeat until someone fails to return a shot or one of you collapses, whichever comes first.

Why You Shouldn't Bother

Absurd as it sounds given the limited space, a doubles version of this game exists. It's only recommended for advanced players, but anyone who remembers what it was like trying to cook a meal in a cramped student kitchen will quickly get a feel for this hugely frustrating variation. Following a little black ball around a pristine white space like it's a fly on a wedding cake is really bad for your eyes, eyes you'll be needing to use on your TV later.

The battle ground for chartered accountants and bank managers.

Sumo Wrestling

To the casual observer, sumo looks like two fat men attempting to give each other wedgies. This might make sense in some bizarre parallel universe were it not for the fact that it would seem the two competitors arrived in the ring having already given themselves wedgies.

Country of Origin: Japan

Possibility of death or serious injury: Despite the brief periods of activity you'll essentially be morbidly obese, with all the health risks and the sweaty arse crack that involves.

Embarrassing clothing: A small linen affair stuffed between the cheeks of your butt. Given the size of competitors' breasts there are moves to introduce sparkly nipple tassels.

Greatest hazard: Being harpooned by Japanese fishermen or floated out to sea by Greenpeace.

People most likely to enjoy it: If you like the idea of playing sport in a big nappy you may want to give sumo a try. Or psychotherapy.

Potential expansion: Fat people fighting should have enormous potential in North America and with only five seconds of "game time" there are lots of opportunities for commercial breaks. "You join us back at the Doshi..."

Expect to hear: "Does my bum look small in this?"

History

Sumo comes from the broad school of Japanese martial arts, and is unique in that it is one that can be successfully done by big fat people. And while technically it's defined as a modern discipline, its history goes back centuries. The death of Hideyoshi in 1589 led to an unsettled period in Japan's history as newly appointed Shogun Ieyasu sought to achieve absolute power by destabilising the influence of regional governors known as daimyos. He did this by insisting they spent every other year at his parliament, and by inviting them to an extensive calendar of Shinto rituals where they were required to wrestle with divine spirits, in return for food, lodging and travel expenses. The constant travelling meant that daimyos had little chance of exerting any influence in their home towns, and despite his promises Ieyasu forced the daimyo to pay their own way, stating that he'd put his wallet down somewhere in the palace but couldn't remember where. The massive changes that occurred during this period in Japan's history were to bring an end to the established social hierarchy and create a class of masterless samurai called ronin who became the first generation of sumo wrestlers. Unlike modern sumo, these mercenaries would roam the land as free agents, answering only to themselves. And with all that roaming they probably weren't so porky either.

You'll Need...

To be enormous. Like most martial arts, sumo is not so much a sport as an entire way of life – and in sumo's case it's a particularly unattractive one. In contrast to the wandering ronin of old, you'll have to live in a stable with a bunch of other big fat guys if you're really serious about it. You'll also have a trainer – or stablemaster – who will assign you a new name. There's no evidence that you have to go out "on the gallops" every morning and get ridden by a midget with an irritating Irish accent, though. Because of the success of Polynesian wrestlers, stables have recently been told they must restrict the number of non-

Matsuko Kawabashi signals his intention to use a jazz hands attack.

Japanese wrestlers in their employ to just one each, so competition for places is actually fiercer amongst foreign wrestlers than ever before. Still interested?

The sacred *dhoyo* – women in Japan are not allowed to touch a sumo's ring.

How You Do It

What you're trying to do is get your opponent to either step or fall out of the ring, or touch the ground with anything other than his feet. Fighters can also lose the bout by having their belts – called mawashi – come completely undone. Which really doesn't bear thinking about.

Advanced

As with many things, the key to the bout is not the brief period of actual wrestling but the pre-match build up. This involves a huge amount of posturing, a large portion of salt throwing and a colossal amount of looking colossal.

Why You Shouldn't Bother

The fact that fighters can spend 20 minutes building up for a bout that's over in three seconds has led many to assert that as far as actual combat goes, sumo is all mouth and no trousers. All too literally.

Surfing

The Polynesians started it, the Beach Boys made it sound glamorous and now surfing is so popular that all the best beach breaks are packed out and violence flares in the lineups. How uncool is that, dude?

Country of Origin: Hawaii

Possibility of death or serious injury: Yes. Sharks love surfers. Particularly in South Africa, California and Australia, where they are known as "the men in grey suits". Both tiger sharks and great whites will attack you, but it is the great whites that like to launch themselves out of the water and bite you in half in a surprise attack. Yum.

Embarrassing clothing: Not in warm climates. In colder climates surfers still have to dress up like seals.

Greatest hazard: Hitting your head on the board, hitting your head on the reef, hitting your head on another surfer. Locals throwing rocks at you because you're surfing at their local break. Getting your surf leash trapped under a submerged rock, being drowned by the sheer weight of water crashing down on your head. Want any more?

Watch out for: All of the above plus jellyfish, effluent and jetskis.

Prize/Rewards: Top competition surfers now attract huge sponsorship deals and can win huge cash prizes. They can also be dragged beneath the waves in a boiling froth of blood just like really crap surfers.

Potential expansion: Surfing has already spawned a host of other sports including kite surfing, wind surfing, urban surfing and, for those who've had far too much to drink, bed surfing.

Expect to hear: "I got spat out the barrel, dude!"

History

The original slacker pursuit was more than just a spot of fun for the ancient Polynesians, whose entire culture was built around the ocean, expert wave riding, and grass skirts twinned with bikini tops made from coconut shells. In 1778 Captain Cook became the first prominent Brit to observe the activity, shortly before he was murdered by the same natives who'd been happily catching big kahunas five minutes before slinging him on the barbie. Which just goes to show surfers aren't all like the laid-back turtle in *Finding Nemo*.

You'll Need...

A two-metre board with a leash so that the only person it does any damage to when you come off it is you. In Europe you'll need a wetsuit with gloves and boots and an understanding with the rest of your party that no one is to take photos, as you'll look a complete idiot. In any part of the world where it's actually enjoyable to be in the water – that has waves – you'll need a six-figure bank balance or a willingness to live on the beach, battle insects and go without eating for a fortnight. And you'll need shark repellent.

How You Do It

Paddle out from the point in the ocean where the waves are breaking. If you're not a strong swimmer, don't worry. Just paddle back to the beach, walk to your hotel's reception and book some swimming lessons. That is unless you're keen on being dragged out to sea on a riptide. Doofus. Now assuming you're OK with the swimming part of the sport, turn so that you're facing the beach and wait for a good wave.

Surfing does at least offer you a chance to reflect on the mistakes you've made in life, mainly the one you made about half an hour ago when you agreed to come surfing in the first place rather than stay in your hammock reading Stephen King and sipping Mai Tais. Rest assured that whatever wave you choose to go with there'll be a better one along just after. Missed opportunities are all part of the fun. Once you've caught a wave, paddle for your life and then, once you're sure it's caught you, keep paddling for an extra 4–6 strokes. Now lift your body into an arched press-up position. Bring the tips of your toes up onto the tail of the board. Gripping the rails (sides) of your board, slide your knees up between your hands and lift your feet onto the board so that your heels are at a 90 degree angle to each other, about 90cm apart, keeping your knees bent. Now release your hands from the rails and slowly bring them up to help you balance. Should you succeed in managing all of the above before you've made it back to shore then radical, dude, you are surfing. Chances are you've already fallen off during the standing up bit. Spit the salt out and try again.

Advanced

Surfers break waves down into categories which you'll need to know and recognise if you're foolish enough to want to advance. Among these are "heavies" (waves that are 12-foot plus in height) "crunchers" (big waves that break hard and are impossible to ride) "shore break" (waves that break close to land and are hard to ride for very long) and "glassy" (smooth water conditions that make surfing very hard – and provide a great excuse for you to take a shore break of your own).

Why You Shouldn't Bother

Surfing was once man's ultimate expression of one-ness with nature. Now it's usually an excuse to rack up more pointless airmiles than a U.N. election observer, and leave a carbon footprint the size of a Chinese power station, as well-heeled surfers chase the ultimate wave. Either that or choose to surf closer to home and battle it out with a million body boarders who don't know the unwritten rules of surfing. Or go to South Africa and combine your surfing holiday with shark feeding.

"Wooahhh, bummer."

Surf Lifesaving

Only the Aussies could take an act of kindness and turn it into a sport. Soon we'll have competitive dog rescuing, pro-celebrity whale refloating and tie me kangaroo down, sport.

Country of Origin: Australia

Possibility of death or serious injury: Oh yes. Just as church-goers can be some of the most un-Christian people in the world, competitive life-savers are vicious and uncaring. They'll drown you to get past you.

Embarrassing clothes: Some say that men in effete little hats look good. Others say that their swim trunks are so tight nobody's looking at their little hats anyway.

Greatest hazard: With the long boat rescue element of a beach carnival, it's having a wave catch your boat and tip you out into the surf like emptying a paper bin. Which kind of ruins the idea of it being a life-saving event and more like a life-endangering event.

Watch out for: Graham Norton. Men with unfeasibly large moustaches.

People most likely to enjoy it: Graham Norton and Allan Carr.

Expect to hear: "Oooooh, chase me, chase me!"

History

Surf lifesaving clubs sprang up on the beaches of Sydney around the turn of the last century after the strict laws prohibiting bathing during daylight hours were relaxed. Everyone rushed into the surf in a frenzy to play that pit-a-pat ball game and there were countless drownings, promoting the need for organized lifeguards. Disputes over who had the bragging rights to be the best surf rescue club soon arose. They were settled by a host of competitions at surf carnivals and include a team launching a traditional lifesaving long boat, rounding a buoy and then getting back to shore again …without spilling a drop of the amber nectar.

You'll Need…

To live near a beach – or a golf course with very large bunkers. Though for practising the long boat element, a sea is useful.

Why You Shouldn't Bother

With windsurfers, surfers and kayakers already crowding out the surf, the beach should remain a sport-free sanctuary. Apart from beach volleyball, of course.

One of the most testing surf rescue disciplines – the lost contact lens in sand.

Sydney–Hobart

It's the elite yachting race of the southern hemisphere. All you need is a $5 million boat plus 400 crew.

Country of Origin: Australia

Possibility of death or serious injury: Yes. People have died on the Sydney–Hobart and there are countless ways to injure yourself on a racing yacht – getting your fingers jammed in the winch, getting knocked unconscious by the boom, terminal sea-sickness, broken masts.

Greatest hazard: It's not unknown for there to be tornadoes in the Bass Strait during the race. And whereas your average landsman will try and avoid one – if it's heading in the right direction, fanatical skippers will sail towards them.

Watch out for: Hobart. Vile mutinies. Falling overboard. Because they might throw you a life raft but they won't stop.

Potential expansion: Loads. The Sydney–Hobart–Sydney. The Sydney–Auckland. The Sydney–Darwin. The Sydney–Sydney (round Australia race) and of course the Sydney–Orlando (aka the Sydney–Disney.

Expect to hear: "Take that ****ing fishing line in!"

History

The Sydney–Hobart race was going to be a gentle cruise down to Tasmania until some interfering Royal Navy officer suggested it might be a lot more fun if Peter Luke and his cruising buddies made it a race. Luke stuck to his guns and cruised there in six days (the slowest ever time) but these days ocean races can make it in one day and 18 hours.

You'll Need…

A boat, a skipper and some hands.

How You Do It

Out of Sydney Harbour. Turn right. Left is wrong, left is Brisbane. After a day you'll see a big island. Head for the left side of it. Round the corner and straight into Hobart. Ignore the packs of inbreds that roam wild on the shores.

Why You Shouldn't Bother

It's run between Christmas and New Year, which completely ruins the Christmas break. Who wants to be rubbing barnacles off a hull when they could be necking some lager in front of televised sport?

Skippers can cut their costs by taking ferry passengers. They also double up as fenders coming into port.

Synchronised Swimming

Is it swimming? Is it art? Is it what happens when you take psychedelic drugs and invent a sport for makeup artists?

Country of Origin: Austria (probably)

Possibility of death or serious injury: Rare, but it has been known. At the 2008 Olympics one of the Japanese competitors suffered hyperventilation in the final and had to be rescued from the pool. A big burly lifeguard rushed in to drag her out of the water, which totally ruined their marks for artistic interpretation.

Embarrassing clothing: You will be wearing a very tight costume and repeatedly opening and closing your legs. So you need to make sure that your swimming costume has the maximum breaking strain...unless you want to make the TV highlights show *100 Most Embarrassing Sporting Moments.*

Watch out for: Casting directors for 1920s and 30s musicals.

Prize/Rewards: A DVD in which everyone looks the same.

People most likely to enjoy it: Young athletic women with long legs, a large lung capacity and an enjoyment of high camp. The ability to apply makeup with a paintbrush is also helpful.

Expect to hear: "You can stop smiling now, this is the changing room."

History

In Ira Levin's seminal 1970s thriller *The Stepford Wives*, a young couple leave New York City and move to a seemingly idyllic community to raise their growing children. At first everything seems just peachy. But the young wife, a model for all that the 1960s had delivered in giving women independence and equality, is concerned by the women of the town, who swan robotically about in revealing floral outfits that leave few details of their athletic bodies to the imagination of the town's men folk, while their smiles are fixed rictus-like to their faces beneath glassy glimmering eyes. Their every move, in short, seems somehow not quite human. All of which brings us to Synchronised Swimming. Levin doesn't go into too much detail about how the women of Stepford keep their spectacular shapes. Well, he sort of does but if you haven't read it I'd hate to spoil the ending for you. In any case, if it were me laying money I'd take any odds you'd care to name that Stepford has its own synchronised swimming club. And if you're female, membership is compulsory.

You'll Need...

A double dose of the X chromosome. The whole sexual equality thing hasn't quite made

Swimmers recreate the lawn sprinkler.

it as far as the sync swimming community, as ze men are completely *verboten*. Ladies, you'll need a nose clip. This will stop the water from going up your nose when you're under it and then cascading out along with a bunch of green stuff as soon as you surface, which tends to undermine the image of glamorous poise you're supposedly trying to represent. You'll also need a swimsuit that matches that worn by your team-mates. I know that would normally cause arguments but you're just going to have to get on with each other as best you can.

How You Do It

The two main skills required of synchronised swimmers are sculling, which is used to propel the body through the water, and egg beating, which is an advanced form of treading water and is used to lift the body out of the water whilst leaving the arms free to perform with. Both of these actions, whilst requiring vast amounts of energy and concentration to execute, should be performed with grace, ease, and, above all, with a smile on your face. In short you'll need to learn how to be a duck. Despite the fact that you have neither wings, feathers, nor webbed feet.

Advanced

In order to project a suitably expressive image most teams employ cosmetic artists to make up

Only the Spanish team could perform Andrew Lloyd-Webber's *Cats*... in water.

their teams before events with special waterproof product ranges. In recent years this has led to allegations that men have snuck their way into competing in events, as most of the contestants come out of the dressing rooms looking like cheap drag acts.

Why You Shouldn't Bother

No one cares. No one watches. Not even your family. They've been lying for years. They record it for you, sure. But when they watch it with you it's the first time they've seen it.

Competitors' smiles must be visible at a distance of five miles – about the height of a meteorological balloon.

Tour de France

The Tour de France is the world's oldest, largest and Frenchest cycling race, and takes place over 21 gruelling stages packed into 23 arse-aching, muscle-shredding, thigh-chafing days.

Country of Origin: Where d'you think?

Possibility of death or serious injury: Serious injuries are rare, but when the peloton (pack) goes down in a high-speed chase there can be carnage. A broken collar bone is the most typical injury along with a variety of abrasions to arms, legs and backsides. Every year a few riders come off the road on fast descents and go over barriers. Lance Armstrong once famously went off the road and cut across a field.

Embarrassing clothing: Men's cycling shorts aren't the most pleasant things to look at, and if yellow so doesn't suit you – remember to go slow. If red polka dots don't suit you – go easy in the mountains.

Watch out for: Mad spectators who have spent all day waiting at the side of the road getting pissed and abusing the riders.

Expect to hear: "C'est les gendarmes! Vite! Cacher les drugs!"

History

The Tour de France remains a truly Gallic event despite the fact that the tour itself regularly takes in diversions through Italy, Spain, Switzerland, Belgium, Luxembourg, Germany, the Netherlands, Ireland and even England. And as you might expect of something so intrinsically French, it all started with an argument. When the Dion car manufacturers fell out with the owners of *Le Velo* newspaper over their position on a soldier found guilty of selling secrets to the Germans, they did what any self respecting mid-to-large company did in those days and started their own rag to peddle their views in. After a typically journalistic liquid lunch on the Montmartre in 1902, the newly appointed *L'Auto's* chief cycling writer came up with the idea of a five-week, round-France cycling race. After coming to – and coming to his senses – he amended his original and somewhat crazy idea to the more manageable, but still frankly a little insane, 19-day event, with the average stage length being around 400km. The shift from offering a contest that promised almost certain death to one which merely guaranteed prolonged periods of total agony proved to be a wise one. The list of registered entrants shot up from a gentleman of no fixed abode, wearing a floral dress and claiming to be Napoleon, to a total of 60 relatively respectable, if foolhardy, individuals. The tour's place in history was assured.

You'll Need…

A bike. Some of those absurd padded lycra shorts that make it look as though you're wearing a designer adult nappy that's in serious need of changing. What you definitely won't need is any kind of drug, be it amphetamines, steroids, uppers, downers, beta blockers, growth hormones, testosterone, or any other banned substance as listed in the World Anti-Doping Agency guidelines. Organisers take allegations about the doping culture of the tour very seriously indeed and whilst the tour has been marred by controversy over drug taking for pretty much the entire 100 plus years of its history, they are well on their way to sorting this out. The Tour de France will be drug-free within the next 50 years. Or so.

The Tour de France is the most popular single sporting event in the world. The French list cycling as their fourth favourite pastime after sex, smoking and shrugging their shoulders.

How You Do It

Tactics may be generally dictated by team managers, but the romance of the contest remains centred on individual riders. And since the French have long been considered the most elegant dressers in Europe, with the Italians a close second and the Welsh a distant 49th, it's no surprise that prowess in the tour is rewarded with a series of natty jerseys – yellow for the overall race leader, a white jersey with red dots for the "king of the mountains" and a "Boo me, I'm rubbish" jersey for whoever's in last place.

Advanced

One of the things that adds further to the particular mystique of the tour is the complex code of conduct that sits alongside the official rules. If it's your birthday you'll be given the chance to lead the stage raced that day. And if the race leader stops for a call of nature, the other racers are expected to stop too. Though in most cases the pressure of having to pee in front of 160 other people often proves too much and merely adds further delay.

Why You Shouldn't Bother

By the time an entrant has completed the Tour de France he'll have travelled a distance you'd worry about achieving in your family car without getting it serviced first, and at comparable speeds. He'll have reached 60mph on downhill descents and ground his way up to mountain-top finishes in temperatures of 33 degrees Centigrade. And did we tell you about the boils on your arse...?

Triathlon

Triathletes are the biggest pain/endorphin junkies in sport. For them, the race is just as much fun as the warm-down whipping afterwards.

Country of Origin: France

Possibility of death or serious injury: It's possible that you'll survive, but you'll have burned so many calories that the lightest touch will snap you like a twig.

Embarrassing clothing: No, the wetsuit then shorts and singlet will complement your frozen rictus of agony nicely.

Prize/Rewards: Like the marathon the reward is considered to be the fact that you've actually completed a triathlon. Readers may like to be reminded that a similar sense of satisfaction can be achieved from doing the crossword or cleaning out the garage.

People most likely to enjoy it: Those who in previous centuries would have been interested in the wearing of hair shirts and self flagellation.

Expect to hear: "Have you seen my other trainer anywhere?"

History

Not one, not two, but three whole kinds of stupid, the modern triathlon comes to us courtesy of those crazy French, presumably as the only means to burn off the vast amount of calories they pack into their butter-, cream- and wine-based cuisine. Adopted by the Californians in the early 1970s and embraced by the Aussies for their Ironman competitions.

You'll Need...

The swimming stages of a triathlon usually take place in open water so a wetsuit is a good idea. Many triathletes opt to just jump straight onto their bikes straight out of the water without getting changed, giving them the appearance as they pedal along of a superhero fallen on hard times. A state-of-the-art racing bike is obviously a must, presumably with an even more state-of-the-art padlock to stop it getting nicked while you're busy drowning in the ocean. Finally, a good pair of running shoes to complete the last stage of the race, though

Each year the Japanese and Norwegians net a large number of triathletes – for scientific purposes.

many first-time competitors tend to find themselves completing the final stage of their first triathlon strapped to a gurney in the back of an ambulance.

How You Do It

Modern triathlon may be the first – and only – sport where competitors are timed and penalised based on how long it takes them to get changed. This may explain why women have traditionally performed poorly compared to their male counterparts. However, it has done little to consolidate the case for including events such as Pro Deciding Which Restaurant to Eat At and Long Distance Arguing Over Whose Turn it is to Drive at the 2012 Olympics.

Advanced

In the *Magnum, P.I.* episode "Beauty Knows No Pain" our eponymous detective shows the world how it should be done. He manages to compete in the Hawaii Ironman – a full distance triathlon covering a 2.4-mile swim, a leisurely 112-mile cycle ride and a full marathon – and solve a missing persons case that's been vexing him throughout his one-week training period and comes out of it with not a moustache hair out of place.

Why You Shouldn't Bother

After 11 hours of punishment, where even stopping to tie a shoelace is considered a waste of time, it's little wonder that the human body starts going into meltdown. If running a marathon is probably not that good for you, then effectively swimming the distance to the horizon and following that up with a push-bike lap of the Paris orbital as a pre-run warm-up is hardly going to help matters. The International Triathlon Union has sanctioned such a growing variety of triathlons it's getting harder to pick an event than order a coffee in Starbucks. Still, there's bound to be one to suit you, whether it's a triathlon-late super sprint (quarter mile swim, 6.2 mile cycle, mile and a half run) or even an Aquabike, sadly not what Aquaman bought for his son's birthday but a two-stage "triathlon" that doesn't include the run. One thing unites all athletes competing in these many and varied hybrids. They're all dismissed by Full Ironman Competitors as being pussies. Unless, of course, you decide to opt for the 320-mile Ultraman variation. In which case, you won't be mocked by anyone. You will, however, be sectioned under the mental health act as soon as you finish the course. That's if the vultures haven't got you first.

Forget the combination on your bike lock and that's your afternoon jiggered.

Triple Jump

Technique is everything in triple jump. If you're one of the unfortunate 30 per cent of the adult population who is lacking the camp gene you may find it impossible to learn and should choose another event.

Country of Origin: Greece?

Possibility of death or serious injury: Triple jumpers usually suffer muscle sprains, tendon injuries and a terminal loss of cool.

Watch out for: Buckets and spades left in your sandpit. Plus what the dog decided to bury.

People most likely to enjoy it: Fans of *Will & Grace*. People for whom one jump is never enough.

Expect to hear: "I've really got to spend some serious time on my skip."

History

The links between sporting prowess and ability in armed conflict are as old and as natural as time itself. The Olympic Games were originally designed as a way for the warriors of ancient Greece to hone their skills and stay in shape during the off-season on butchering Trojans. It's for this reason that so many of the events we all enjoy witnessing at the modern Olympics test abilities that would have been highly prized in a time of war, such as javelin (for spear throwing); pole-vaulting (for getting over the enemy's battlements); shot putt (a bit of harmless fun with the heads of your enemy); and 400m sprint (for getting off the battlefield once you've realised that the Trojans are actually a bit tasty in a fight). All of which brings us to the triple jump, formerly known as the hop, skip and jump.

You'll Need...

Leaving aside the fact that you'll look a total and utter prat doing it for just one moment, it's worth considering the few positive things that triple jumping has going for it. The main one is that it's a very cheap sport to get involved in. You won't need any specialist kit beyond normal track wear. Although given the somewhat ridiculous nature of what you're about to do you might want to try really styling it out and go for the so-nerdy-you're-almost-cool *Napoleon Dynamite* look by teaming the most unflattering shorts and vest you can with a pair of vintage plimsolls and knee-high grey socks. And glasses held together with a sticking plaster.

How You Do It

It's a hop, it's a girly skip and then it's a jump. Hope by that time you've at least reached the edge of the sandpit.

Why You Shouldn't Bother

Like being the least hairy girl at an Amish wedding, champion triple jumpers may not necessarily cut much of a figure outside the goldfish bowl of their own immediate circle. And no matter how good you may or may not get at it, you'll always look like a puddle-jumping weirdo.

The family of this athlete has no idea that he triple jumps at weekends. They think he goes to the beach a lot.

Tug of War

It involves a lot of straining and a lot of grunting, whilst lying back and tugging hard. Tug of war is the closest anyone gets to having sex in public.

Country of Origin: Egypt

Possibility of death or serious injury: Not unless you live in mortal fear of getting your hands grazed by knotty hemp. Alternatively, if both teams are either side of a ravine…

Embarrassing clothing: No, that remains reserved for the Morris Dancers.

Greatest hazard: Attempting it in a pair of flip flops.

Watch out for: Crude and pathetic jokes involving the word "anchor".

People most likely to enjoy it: Big, jolly chaps at a summer fête, after about six hours in the beer tent.

Expect to hear: "On the count of three, everybody let go."

History

The first games of tug of war were probably played by Egyptians as a break from the stresses and strains of building the pyramids. Although the role the Egyptians took in the sport was almost certainly more of a managerial one, the actual donkey work of pulling the rope being done by their Hebrew slaves, while opposing Egyptian supervisors whipped up (quite literally) some encouragement for the break-time activity. Since then it's a sport that's been played and enjoyed by millions all over the world, and may be one of the only sports where pie-eating, salad-dodging lard-arses come into their own.

You'll Need…

A rope, marked at the centre with paint, tape or, if you're a country and western fan, a yellow ribbon. You'll also need friends to play it with. One on one is an option, although from the outside it's less likely to resemble a game of tug of war as a slightly bizarre domestic disturbance. Ideally you'll be able to muster up two teams of eight, with the heaviest player taking the position at the furthest rear end of the rope, a role traditionally known as the "anchor", which, rather predictably, is always a source of great fun for their team-mates. A lot more fun than the game they're about to participate in anyway.

Advanced

In order to spice things up for contestants some events will involve the use of a "penalty zone" moat filled with soft earth, or water, or angry crayfish.

Why You Shouldn't Bother

Tug of war may be many things, but one thing it isn't is strategically complex. Whilst this may explain its huge popularity in South Africa's rugby-playing regions, it leaves commentators and pundits struggling to justify their presence in covering events. "So, Richie, what do you see as being the tactics for this next match?" "Well, Troy, I think that both teams are going to get in there and pull as hard as they can…"

Tug of War. The refuge of elite pie munchers the world over.

179

Underwater Hockey

Underwater hockey is often referred to as "Octopush" by enthusiasts and "What did you do that for?" by just about everybody else.

Country of Origin: The Lost Kingdom of Atlantis

Possibility of death or serious injury: Drowning, though uncommon, has been known. Unlike field hockey and ice hockey, goalminders don't need Kevlar pads and facemasks, just some Speedos with the letter G.

Embarrassing clothing: No need to feel embarrassed as nobody ever watches.

Greatest hazard: Getting a team up. Or should that be down.

Watch out for: People sniggering behind their hands.

Prize/Rewards: At the pinnacle of your underwater hockey career you might be presented with a small plastic trophy in the changing room after leading your team to victory in the world championships.

People most likely to enjoy it: Are very rare. Failed synchronised swimmers who couldn't get to grips with the whole floating/buoyancy thing.

Potential expansion: Over the next million or so years, experts hope that underwater hockey might evolve into the baby pool and eventually onto dry land.

Expect to hear: "Glarrg – grrrrg – glaargg – you bastard!"

History

Underwater hockey was originally invented in the 1950s as a way of keeping members of the British sub aqua club in the water during the long and generally bitter U.K. winters and thus accelerating their human gill evolution programme. Forty-four teams from 17 countries competed at the World Championships in Sheffield in 2006, and while the homo sapien species is still waiting to evolve gills, there is at least evidence that he is finally and belatedly evolving some common sense, since the entry level for the 2008 Underwater Hockey World Championships was marked by fewer entries than a Zimbabwean election.

You'll Need...

A hockey stick for each player. Underwater hockey sticks are unusually small, and should measure no more than 35cm in length. That's about the size of a toothbrush you'd use on a horse. Finally, a puck made of one and a half kilogrammes of lead, covered in a plastic coating. Almost like a treat you'd give to a well-behaved robot.

How You Do It

Teams of 6–10 players compete to get the puck into their opponent's goal. Despite being made of one of the densest elements known to man,

Underwater hockey: Where the excitement never starts.

Mid-game snacks are often thrown on the surface of the water.

the heavyweight puck can actually be lofted during the execution of a pass, although if you pass it too close to an opponent's head you're likely to have a foul awarded against you. The biggest danger won't come from the puck though, but from the constant head banging you'll endure as you rise to the surface for air only to meet your fellow players on their way back down to the action, and vice versa. The sensation of crashing into some idiot that wasn't looking where they were going will be all too familiar to anyone who's actually tried swimming lengths in a public pool.

Advanced

Obviously one of the key reasons this remains a minority sport – other than its inherent stupidity – is the fact that few of us are lucky enough to have our own swimming pool. However, most public pools can be hired out for a reasonable sum at off-peak times. You better warn the lifeguard, though, because he's going to be diving in every five minutes to hook you off the bottom.

Why You Shouldn't Bother

Even in a senseless world like our own where evil deeds go unpunished every day, food is destroyed while millions starve and Mel Gibson is still given money to make movies, underwater hockey has scaled new heights of inexplicable pointlessness. The best thing to recommend underwater hockey as a sport is that it's virtually impossible to watch as a spectator, so there's no danger of one of your friends dragging you along to see them compete. Unless some wily promoter comes up with the idea of staging the next World Championships at Seaworld in Florida, and forces the teams to share their arena with Shamu the Killer Whale. Or introduces blunt-nosed-but-still-mildly-uncomfortable harpoons as a defensive aid, (think underwater paintball) that might just make this sport both easy and enjoyable to watch for the first time in its history.

Someone's hypnotised them and told them it's a box of chocolates.

Unicycle Hockey

There comes a moment in every Unicycle Hockey player's life when they wake up in the middle of the night clutched with the chill knowledge that they're not crazy and funny, they're a twat.

Country of Origin: Germany

Possibility of death or serious injury: As might be expected, the history of unicycling is one of discomfort, awkwardness, bruised shins and broken scaphoids.

Embarrassing clothing: Contrary to expectations you don't have to wear a big red wig and nose.

People most likely to enjoy it: Hippies labouring under the misapprehension that circus skills are cool. Like lion taming and juggling seals? No way, man.

Prize/Rewards: Sweet FA of course.

History

Bizarre as it may seem, the commonly accepted origin of the unicycle is a mode of transport even less practical and even more likely to put its rider in traction: the Penny Farthing. In many ways the world's mass-produced vehicular death-trap, the Penny Farthing was a bicycle with pedals which were connected directly to the front wheel. Since this could measure anything up to one and a half metres this gave the rider an elevated position from which to observe other road traffic, though the road such as it was would be an uneven track at best and a puddle strewn mudfest at worst. The only advantage of such conditions being that the rider would at least be guaranteed a relatively soft, if somewhat messy, landing, when his short time in control of this unpredictable contraption came to an inevitably premature

end. It wasn't until the following century that the customisers got hold of it and created a sawn-off low-rider unicycle to be enjoyed the world over... in circus rings.

You'll Need...

A unicycle. Most players use freestyle bikes, which have a higher than usual seatpost, a squared fork, and cotter-less cranks. But still just the one wheel. Unicycle hockey is, astonishingly, still something of a minority sport, so it's yet to get its own section in your sports supply shop. So you'll need a standard ice hockey stick and a tennis ball.

Why You Shouldn't Bother

Unicycle hockey differs from ice hockey in that it isn't merely an excuse for a fight. Given its tendency to be played by members of the circus skills/clowning fraternity, violence as a result of disputed decisions is very rare, and when it does occasionally break out it is usually no more than a brief exchange of buckets of water (actually filled with glitter), or an exchange of blows with a large rubber mallet.

A few anti-personnel mines might liven it up.

(Beach) Volleyball

For many around the world, beach volleyball is the very apogee of competitive achievement. It has pace. It has drama. It has young women in small bikinis writhing around the floor then kissing each other.

Country of Origin: USA

Possibility of death or serious injury: The sport can have tragic consequences. After two weeks of olympic coverage, some male commentators have been known to have a stroke.

Embarrassing clothing: Small, tight costumes for women are nothing but liberating. Men should be made to wear the same to establish parity.

Watch out for: The one who's not serving reminding the server what a "mighty fine arse" they've got.

People most likely to enjoy it: Healthily tanned women between the ages of 18 and 24, for whom the sport should be mandatory. Freckly gingas were banned from the sport in 1986 on health risk grounds.

Potential expansion: It would be nice to see the debut of mudbath volleyball, marshmallow pit volleyball and foamy lather/bouncy castle volleyball.

History

Like surfing, beach volleyball originated in Hawaii, at The Outrigger Club where bored surfers passed the time when the waves weren't pumpin'. It transferred to Southern California in the 1920s and grew from there.

You'll Need...

No cellulite, a swimsuit that's too small and a team-mate that's not as good-looking as you.

How You Do It

You serve the ball over a net and try and lob the ball into your opponents' court. They mustn't let it touch their sand and have three touches to get it back. If you score a point, you must touch your team-mate in some way, a playful slap of the bottom, or a hi-five is usually enough. At the end of the game you hug your team-mate and roll on the sand with her for five minutes.

Why You Shouldn't Bother

This isn't a sport for biffas, gingas, munters and mingers. It's for beautiful people. Please don't dilute the gene pool.

Yeah, all right, we've seen it.

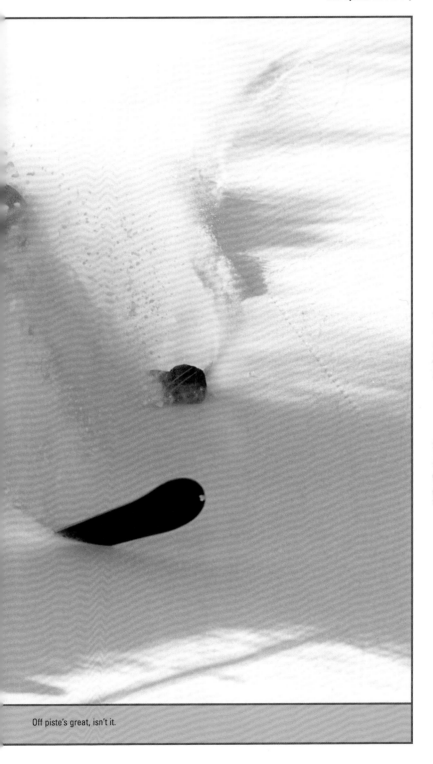

Off piste's great, isn't it.

Water Polo

The big question that hangs over the sorry sport of water polo is why it isn't played on horseback, as this would make it all a lot more entertaining for the spectators, though the pool might need a bit of a clean afterwards.

Country of Origin: Scotland

Possibility of death or serious injury: Low, if you remember to take your arm bands.

Watch out for: A spectator. If one appears, play should be stopped while it is explained that they won't be able to swim until the match has finished.

Prize/Rewards: Interestingly, this is an Olympic sport so there are gold medals to be won.

Potential expansion: It's thought that the five minutes of media attention water polo receives every four years is already five minutes too many.

History

We can all remember the first time we experienced the fascinating combination of holding a ball in a body of water. The simple joy of expending a massive force on it in a futile attempt to keep it submerged. The glee that came when it was finally released from its watery confines and allowed to fly unimpeded and then splash back down on the water before bobbing off on its merry way. Of course, the excitement wears off fairly quickly, but it's all good fun for a few minutes. Which is a lot more than can be said for a game of water polo, a sport that takes the simple activity of playing throw and catch in the pool and turns it into a dull game that manages to be totally exhausting for everyone participating.

You'll Need...

A 30-metre pool, a ball and six similarly misguided individuals to make up the rest of your team. Above all you'll need the lungs of an opera singer and the constitution of a superhero. Some players will also choose to wear two sets of briefs for extra security.

How You Do It

Perhaps the most striking feature of water polo is that with the exception of the two goalies, teams are not organised by positions. This has led to suggestions that the England football squad form a water polo team as this will clearly play to one of their few strengths.

Why You Shouldn't Bother

Water polo is played in four quarters of seven minutes. That might seem like a fairly short length of time for an event. But when you've spent even one minute tearing from one end of the pool to the other in pursuit of a ball you're only ever allowed to hold with one hand, egg beating to lift yourself out of the water and engaging in wrestling bouts with your opposite numbers, frankly you'll soon realise that the game can't be over quickly enough.

Such an uncanny resemblance to land polo.

Wife Carrying

Having carried their new wife over the threshold, many men stop there. A small minority seem to enjoy it so much they made a sport out of it. A sport that is now so competitive that there are an extraordinary number of marriages taking place between Scandinavian men and anorexic midgets.

Country of Origin: Finland

Possibility of death or serious injury: You should be fine so long as you remember to take her out to dinner afterwards.

Embarrassing clothing: There's no approved kit so wear something simple that will accessorize well with a fully-grown woman across the shoulders. You may wish to try a few before you find one that you're comfortable with. Size 8 is good, size 16+ and your vertebrae will fuse.

Greatest hazard: Being caught carrying your neighbour's wife. "I was only practising for the race", is a very thin excuse, especially if you were giving *her* the post-race rub-down.

Watch out for: Difficult to navigate hazards, such as water-filled ditches, fences and shoe shops.

Prize/Rewards: Traditionally the prize awarded to the winner is the wife's weight in beer, giving rise to the equation that the value of the prize available rises in inverse proportion to the likelihood of winning it.

Potential expansion: Recent experiments to cut out the middle man (or woman) and make it a beer carrying competition proved shortlived as no one bothered to carry the beer further than their living room.

Expect to hear: "Don't fancy yours much."

History

In recent years we've come to know the Scandinavians as producers of about 95 per cent of the global student bedsit furniture, as well as the home of some of the world's most beautiful, glacially superior women and, conversely, the ugliest drunk-by-noon men. We've questioned their commitment to the Geneva Convention in the alleged atrocities they've committed against the herring community. And we've marvelled at their ability to speak eight languages, ski the length of a marathon before breakfast and maintain a pleasant and polite disposition in the face of sweeping generalisations and cheap gags made by idiot authors. But in considering their cultural development its worth noting that geography, whilst giving them a bunch of nice looking fjords, has not been kind to them, especially in socio-political terms. Despite some good times looting and pillaging in the dark ages, and playing a major role in the shaping of Europe before 1400, the Scandinavians have spent most of the last five hundred years between a rock and a hard place – the rock being Russia in its many and various forms, and the hard place being the Baltic Sea which is frozen over during the bleak winter. Perhaps it's for that reason that Scandinavians have learnt to find fun in the most unlikely of acts – watching repeats of Benny Hill, jumping into icy pools naked, and inventing odd sports like wife carrying.

You'll Need...

A wife. If you have trouble locating one of these by conventional methods they can be found cheaply and quickly on the Internet.

Check the seller's ebay rating first. Of course it doesn't have to be *your* wife, it only has to be *a* wife.

How You Do It

Different nationalities have adopted favoured approaches to the techniques that lie at the heart of this inane sport. An over-the-shoulder fireman's style lift seems to be the preferred method for most northern Scandinavians, while the Estonians practise a hold where wifey's legs go around her husband's neck and she hangs upside down with her arms around his hips, which has been banned from use in several competitions on the grounds of moral decency.

Advanced

Whichever method of carrying you and your spouse choose to adopt, you need to practise in order to stand any chance of winning. Wife carrying may sound like a bit of fun, but the standard in most competitions is now incredibly high. There is even Ironman Wife Carrying where contestants drag their wives a mile through water on a rubber wing, sling her across the crossbar of a bike for a five-mile ride and then finish off with the traditional run. Influential gay groups have queried the whole name of the sport in Sweden where it has been renamed Life Partner Carrying. In liberal countries such as Holland it is now called Significant Other Carrying, while in San Francisco it is called Giving a Lift to a Friend of Dorothy. An increasing number of Australian men are taking up the sport following complaints from their wives that they didn't take them out enough.

Why You Shouldn't Bother

Despite an excellent and very tempting prize you'll need a wife with a great sense of humour and physical stamina who's very fond of you and doesn't mind giving up valuable shopping time to train for a pointless event. Since all of that is unheard of for anyone who has been married for more than two weeks it's unlikely that you'll even make it to the starting line.

Wife carrying doesn't need to be competitive. You can do it at an amateur level to see how much fun it is. Then stop.

Yabbie Racing

If you want a serious bet on the Melbourne Cup the best thing to do is to "yabbie" it first.

Country of Origin: Australia

Possibility of death or serious injury: Yabbie handling is not for the faint-hearted and their claws should be bound up if you leave them in a tank together. Otherwise, come race day you'll end up with one scarred racing yabbie and seven main courses.

Greatest hazard: Under-supplied seafood chefs.

Watch out for: Ringers. A racing crab dressed up as a yabbie – easy to spot as they only go sideways.

Expect to hear in the future: "Groundhog day" has become the universal phrase for something happening over and over again. Organisers hope that with the popularity of yabbie racing on the rise, it will become a good way to predict forthcoming events and fall into everyday usage – i.e. "Let's not guess, let's go and yabbie it".

History

Yabbie racing is like Australia's equivalent of *Groundhog Day*. In the film starring Bill Murray and Andie MacDowell, the Groundhog – Punxsutawney Phil – is brought out in February each year and if he casts a shadow, then the town of Punxsutawney in Philadelphia is set for six more weeks of winter. The Aussie version is a crayfish race run the day before the Melbourne Cup and yabbies are given the names of the horses running in the race. On three out of six occasions the yabbie has predicted the winner – which probably makes it more accurate than most racing tipsters.

You'll Need...

A stable of racing yabbies. If you wanted to make it even more realistic and have little shrimp jockeys... then you can sod right off. Who's bothered enough to give the crayfish little saddles?

Why You Shouldn't Bother

Like cows, pigs, sheep, chicken and ducks, they're better eaten than raced.

A frisky, two-year-old thoroughbred racing yabbie, in the colours of Sheikh Yerbardi.

Zorbing™

NASA spent millions of dollars training their astronauts in high-speed centrifuges and state-of-the-art machinery, when all they needed was a hill and a big roll of bubble wrap.

Country of Origin: New Zealand

Possibility of death or serious injury: There's a medium to high risk of "Humpty Dumptying", depending on your chosen terrain.

Prize/Rewards: Like bungee jumping the only reward is the cessation of extreme discomfort when it's all over. Plus the ability to say: "I've zorbed".

People most likely to enjoy it: Computer nerds from Athens, who will become known as Zorber the Geek forever more. Sorry. I'll get my coat.

Potential expansion: Further sports inspired by pets include the Underwater Castle Swim-By, the Annual Ball of Wool Steeplechase and the ever-popular Hanging from a Cage by Your Teeth, also known as the Iron Hamster event.

History

The urge to imitate other forms of life is in many ways one borne of nature. Just as men wear stacked heels and stuff socks down their pants to appear more appealing, several species of spider have evolved colourings of striking similarity to surrounding fauna that insects are naturally drawn to, making them easy prey. The harmless mimic octopus can contort its body shape and even alter its own colouring to imitate a venomous sea snake, in the same way that a wannabe gangster rapper can adopt an absurd druggie name and write songs about gats and hoes to cover up his sweet suburban upbringing. And of course playing possum isn't just the preserve of possums anymore, and in the sport of football

overpaid prima donnas have learnt that rolling around simulating the kind of agony they'd experience if they'd just had their leg hacked off at the knee joint is a great way to get their colleagues from the other side a booking. But the question of why on earth anyone would want to imitate a hamster is one that's only occurred fairly recently. The answer may well lie in a detailed analysis of the collective psyche of the people of New Zealand, which we sadly don't have time for here.

You'll Need...

A double-hulled sphere approximately 10 feet in diameter, and fashioned in a transparent material if you'd like to have some sense of where the hell you're going and don't want this to be the land-based equivalent of going down Niagara Falls in a barrel. There are two schools of thought on how the Zorber should interact with the interior of the capsule, with many regular users opting for the safety and security provided by straps to hold onto, a harness to hold you in place and a vomit bag dispenser on hand, while many purists argue that the experience of Zorbing is not complete if you are not free to run around within the ball. Both of these schools miss the point that you're an idiot if you get into one of these at all.

How You Do It

The decision on whether to go for the trussed up tightie whitie approach or adopt a commando style, let it all shake around, philosophy will greatly affect your experience of Zorbing, but ultimately have little effect on the overall outcome of your experience. The former will give you the sensation of being strapped to a medieval torture wheel just before the instruments come out, while the latter will allow you a rare opportunity to empathise with your laundry next time you take it out of the drier.

Advanced

In response to inexplicably high demand, the Zorb franchise has recently diversified to offer thrill seekers a water-based version of their nausea inducing device. The good news here is that unlike the hapless journalist who had her back fractured riding a land Zorb in Maine, you're not so likely to break any bones. Drowning is always an option though.

Why You Shouldn't Bother

If you start your day at the gym running on a treadmill, and follow that up with a breakfast of oats and dried fruit, you're probably spending too much time pretending to be a small rodent already. The net effect of Zorbing can be achieved for a much smaller outlay by drinking cheap cider all day and then standing on your head for five minutes (take the change out of your pockets first). As adrenalin-rush experiences go, the Kiwis have a lot more to offer than a quick Zorb; there are jetboat rides, white water rafting, and not forgetting Megan the Sheep. She won't forget you...

Like a journey down a Fallopian tube, but a lot faster.

Picture Acknowledgements

2. iStockphoto / 5. Reuters/CORBIS / 6. (top) AFP/Getty Images; (bottom) iStockphoto/Joe Stone / 8. Andre Gravel/iStockphoto / 9. Mikhail Kondraskov/iStockphoto / 10. (top) David Touchstone/iStockphoto / 10. iStockphoto / 11. Curtis J.Morley/iStockphoto / 12. (top) John Schulte/iStockphoto / 12. Bill Grove/iStockphoto / 13. Sasha Radosavljevic/iStockphoto / 14. (top) Jim Jurica/iStockphoto / 14. Julie Johnson/iStockphoto / 16. Ann Clark/iStockphoto / 17. Ann Clark/iStockphoto / 18. Matthew Scherf/iStockphoto / 19. Anova Image Library / 20. Christophe Michot/iStockphoto / 21. Christophe Michot/iStockphoto / 22. Corbis / 24. Nicholas Moore/iStockphoto / 25. James Steidl/iStockphoto / 27. Corbis / 29. Corbis / 30. Corbis / 31. Liz Leyden/iStockphoto / 32. Lisa Fletcher/iStockphoto / 34. Bryan Kennedy/iStockphoto / 35. Corbis / 36. iStockphoto / 37. (top) Ryan Johnson/iStockphoto; (bottom) Anova Image Library/David Watts / 39. Corbis / 41. Corbis / 43. (top) Corbis; (bottom) Corbis / 44. Corbis / 45. i-Stockphoto / 46. Bjorn Barton-Pye/iStockphoto / 47. Sheldon Kralstein/iStockphoto / 48. Mark Evans/iStockphoto / 49. iStockphoto / 50. iStockphoto / 51. Corbis / 52. Sam Sefton/iStockphoto / 53. Jason Lugo/iStockphoto / 54. Rober Young/iStockphoto / 57. iStockphoto / 58. iStockphoto / 59. iStockphoto / 61. Corbis / 63. Corbis / 64. iStockphoto / 65. Brane Bozic/iStockphoto / 67. Niki Crucillo/iStockphoto / 69. (top) Hanna Melbye-Hansen/iStockphoto; (bottom) i-Stockphoto / 70. Dejan Sarman/iStockphoto / 71. Dejan Sarman/iStockphoto / 72. Rob Friedman/iStockphoto / 73. Volker Kreinache/iStockphoto / 74. Galina Barskaya/iStockphoto / 75. (top) Trevor Neilson/iStockphoto; (bottom) iStockphoto / 77. Corbis / 78. Alan Crawford/iStockphoto / 79. Duncan Moody/iStockphoto / 80. Christine Balderas/iStockphoto / 81. Rene Mansi/iStockphoto / 82. iStockphoto / 83. Jamie Garrison/iStockphoto / 85. iStockphoto / 87. iStockphoto / 89. Piotr Sikora/iStockphoto / 92. Gregor Erdmann/iStockphoto / 93. James Johnson/iStockphoto / 95. Corbis / 96. Krzysztof Chrystowski/iStockphoto / 97. Eric Gevaert/iStockphoto / 98. iStockphoto / 99. Chad Natkchareon/iStockphoto / 100. i-Stockphoto / 101. Corbis / 102. Corbis / 104. Corbis / 105. Corbis / 106. Tor Lindquist/iStockphoto / 107. Devin Allpkin/iStockphoto / 108. Rick Rhay/iStockphoto / 109. Scott Hailstone/iStockphoto / 110. Corbis / 112. iStockphoto / 113. Eliza Snow/iStockphoto / 114. Corbis / 115. Rick Donovan/iStockphoto / 116. Getty Images / 118. (top) Sascha Burkard/iStockphoto; (bottom) Jurgen Konig/iStockphoto / 119. Brandon Alms/iStockphoto / 120. Bradley Mason/iStockphoto / 122. Anthony Brown/iStockphoto / 123. Richard Schmon/iStockphoto / 124. Corbis / 126. Robert Young/iStockphoto / 127. Joshue Lurie-Terrell/iStockphoto / 128. (top) Dan Brandenburg/iStockphoto / iStockphoto / 129. iStockphoto / 131. Corbis / 132. Corbis / 133. i-Stockphoto / 134. Corbis / 135. iStockphoto / 137. Hasan Shaheed/iStockphoto / 138. i-Stockphoto / 139. Rick Hyman/iStockphoto / 141. Corbis / 142. iStockphoto / 143. Graeme Purdy/iStockphoto / 144. Corbis / 145. Corbis / 146. Corbis / 148. Corbis / 149. iStockphoto / 150. iStockphoto / 151. Joerg Reimann/iStockphoto / 152. (top) Vlado Janzekovi/iStockphoto; (bottom) Holger Gogolin/iStockphoto / 154. iStockphoto / 155. Michalle Gali/iStockphoto / 156. (top) Jason Lugo/iStockphoto; (bottom) Galina Barskaya/iStockphoto / 157. iStockphoto / 158. (top) Sami Suni/iStockphoto; (bottom) Michael Krinke/iStockphoto / 160. (top) Bartosz Liszkowski/iStockphoto; (bottom) Corbis / 161. iStockphoto / 162. Corbis / 163. iStockphoto / 164. Slobo Mita/iStockphoto / 165. Michel Pettigrew/iStockphoto / 167. (top) Troy Kennedy/iStockphoto; (bottom) Bart Parren/iStockphoto / 169. iStockphoto / 170. Corbis / 171. Corbis / 172. Corbis / 173. (top) Corbis; (bottom) Corbis / 175. Daniel Sainthorant/iStockphoto / 176. Corbis / 177. Corbis / 178. iStockphoto / 179. Sue Colvil/iStockphoto / 181. Corbis / 182. iStockphoto / 183. iStockphoto / 184. Corbis / 186. Ferran Traite Soler/iStockphoto / 188. iStockphoto / 189. Chris Adams/iStockphoto / 191. Philippa Banks/iStockphoto.